P9-EMO-987

FUNDAMENTALS

OF

FAMILY COUNSELING

FUNDAMENTALS

OF

FAMILY COUNSELING

A Primer on Learning and Teaching
a Family-Focused Approach

LEON LUCAS, ACSW, Ph.D.

Professor & Chairman of the Social Casework Sequence
Wayne State University

RUTH L. GOLDBERG, ACSW

Associate Professor in the School of Social Work
Wayne State University

Publishers/WHITEHALL COMPANY
601 Skokie Blvd./Northbrook, Ill.

TO OUR SPOUSES AND OUR FAMILIES

WHO EXPANDED OUR UNDERSTANDING OF
FAMILIES AND ASSISTED US IN MANIFOLD
WAYS IN THIS ENDEAVOR

INTRODUCTION

The Role of Family Counseling in Social Work

Anthropological, cultural and social studies have shown that the family in some form is found in every society. Parental, sexual and other roles are institutionalized in small nuclear groups as well as in extended kinship systems. This is a universal characteristic found in all societies and the family system is related to all other units of the social system.

Because of this it is obvious that social work which is concerned with the social functioning of individuals, families, small groups, communities and other levels of society needs to be concerned with the family as one of the major social systems affecting the welfare of society and its members. Social case work, which provides a method of therapeutic intervention for individuals and families unable to cope with necessary life tasks because of external and internal difficulties, obstacles, conflicts, deficits, and excesses in the social system, is concerned with the social functioning of families. Hence, it is understandable that in the course of the evolution of the social case work method the family has always occupied a central role in its concerns and in its preoccupation.

A family is usually defined as a group of individuals related to one another by blood, by the sharing of resources, by legal arrangement, by social arrangement, sharing a shelter or home. Usually the interrelationships among the members of the family are in a higher degree of intensity than they have with members outside the family. Otto Pollak   pointed out that family closeness is determined not only by proximity or blood relationship but rather by the intensity of the relationship and the attitudes about these relationships. The family is viewed as a social system in microcosm and has its subsystems composed of either generational groupings, associational groupings, or intergenerational groupings. Otto Pollak has further succinctly defined the family as a social organization representing a working system of living and development among people of different sex and different stages of physical and mental maturity. Like other social systems of larger scale, it requires norms of behavior which in the last analysis represent an expression of the victory of the reality principle over the pleasure principle." Pollak has also described the different functions of the family as consisting (1) of the emotional function, such as the interpersonal emotional relationships in which need satisfactions are met, (2) biological and social completion idea for personal self-maximization of these aspects, (3) the sexual function, (4) the economic function, and (5) the ego strengthening or supportive function in normal growth and development of the individuals in the family. The family also is a place where individuals learn their social role both as members of the family and as part of the general socialization process.

Social Work,[2] which is an enabling and supportive discipline working towards enchancing social functioning, has in the social case work method a major approach to furthering the development of social intervention methods and processes which support the functioning of families in their growth and development. Social work aims to remove obstacles to such functioning, to repair damage, to enhance functioning and give support to such functioning. Thus, it is aimed at either repairing, restoring or enhancing social functioning of the family. As a basic building block in our social structure, social work considers it extremely important to make a maximum contribution to the greatest realization of the functioning of the families which come as units of attention to the social work enterprise. The individual, of course, is assisted through the medium of the family as well as by direct intervention in behalf of the individual and indirectly in behalf of the family and by other social interventions, manipulations, modifications, and supports.

Leon G. Stubbings of the Australian Red Cross in a paper presented at the International Conference on Social Welfare, Helsinki, Finland in August, 1968 pointed out that we find in general from intercultural experience that kinship and tribal relationships break down as a result of increasing urbanization in a highly industrialized society. Therefore, because of the repetitive experiences in this respect he suggested that we should take steps towards avoiding such destruction of the social provision which in more primitive societies were provided by the extended family and which now we have had to provide increasingly in our industrialized society at large. Insofar as we are able to maintain the socializing and supportive functions of the family we will lessen the need for making social provision otherwise. Because of the rapidly increasing urbanization in our societies there are detrimental effects on family life due to mobility which dilutes and weakens families, breaks up their unity which in turn brings on vagrancy, delinquency, long term separation of husbands and wives and other family members, and rapid economic development which forces families to adjust to a money economy as we move from a subsistence economy. Therefore, we need to take this into account as we meet the urbanization process in ever increasing proportions all over the world. Also external influences such as publicly provided education and mass media of communication move the child to think for himself and, therefore, weaken family ties and add to intergenerational conflict. Thus, we must be aware of the problems which urbanization brings. We have to take measures to counteract it and to minimize its destructive effects on family life. The community must not only develop the community at large but also offer guidance to families on marriage, child care, family life education, home management, nutrition, the role of men and women, health care and other sustaining functions in the general socialization and maturational process through which all individuals move.

Helping the Individual Via the Medium of the Family

Most individuals in our society live in families. It has been noted by D. W. Clark[3] that 94% of the population live in families in the U.S.A. Also the vast majority of the population were married; almost three-quarters of the population over 14 were married. Ninety per cent were married at some point in their life; more Americans are marrying now than ever before; even though the divorce rate is rapidly increasing this is compensated for by the high rate of remarriages after divorce. As individuals live longer, the family also lasts for longer periods of time and children tend to be in the same generational group, being born mainly within 2-1/2 years of each other. Family life is universal as noted in cross-cultural studies. Also we note from cross-cultural studies that (1) usually the family provides strong ties to a maternal person, especially in the early years; (2) monogamy is present in some form because in most societies the number in each sex tends to be more or less equal and also for economic and social reasons; (3) unregulated promiscuity is not characteristic and is usually regulated in some manner; and (4) the family usually has four major functions namely, procreation, orientation, division of labor of the sexes, and status giving.

The basic nature of family stems from the fact that anthropologists, for example, have noted that the human social systems are based in man's psychobiological needs for meeting the basic drives of food, sex and sometimes aggression, and the need for reduction of these drives; these organic needs for food, clothing and shelter and other constitutional needs require learning methods of protection and adaptation. The relatively permanent bi-parental nature of the family as the basis of procreation is due to man's prolonged primate dependency and his continuous sexual drive. This underlies the need for continuous existence of the family over long periods of time. It also serves as the basis for the larger collectivities of societies which involve more than one family and require more permanent social arrangements, including social interaction, methods of social cooperation and techniques of conflict resolution. [4]

In view of the central role of the family in our culture and in our society, the focus of social work has been shifting to the family in interventions in behalf of the individual and the family such as through the social case work method and the use of the family counseling process.

Teaching Family Counseling in Professional Education

In view of the above-mentioned shift of emphasis and the contributions of the social sciences in the past several decades which have given us increasing understanding of small group theory, of family theory, and of family dynamics, new insights and bases for understanding and for developing treatment modalities to deal with family dysfunctioning and social interaction have been made available. These contributions have been gradually introduced into the curriculum in professional education for the preparation of family counselors. This is also related to the broader concerns of social work with the social functioning of communities and social groups insofar as each of these levels of social systems contributes to the maintenance, and growth and development of the family as a social system and enhances the social functioning of all aspects of society, including the individual, the family and the community. This book is intended to provide a description of some of the theoretical bases and the ingredients of the family counseling process and method, and the social processes involved as they have been developed from the experience of the profession and as reported in the rapidly growing literature in this field. Also, we have included the experience of the authors in the practice, study, and teaching of family counseling.

Footnotes

1. Otto Pollak, Social Determinants of Family Behavior, **Social Work**, July 1963, Vol. 8, No. 3, pp. 95-101

2. See definition in **Social Work Curriculum Study**, Council on Social Work Education, 1959, Vol. I, p. 54.

3. D. W. Clark, Family as a Focal Point in Health Education, **Contemporary Society**, edited by I. Galdston (Hallmark Press, New York, 1958).

4. Melford E. Spiro, "Social Systems, Personality, Functional Analysis" in Studying personality Cross-Culturally, Edited by B. Kaplan, Rowe Peterson & Co., Evanston, Illinois, 1961, p. 95.

TABLE OF CONTENTS

Page

CONTENTS

FUNDAMENTALS
OF
FAMILY COUNSELING

SECTION I

FAMILY THEORY AND SOCIAL
WORK PRACTICE

CHAPTER I

THE DYNAMIC ROLE OF FAMILY COUNSELING IN ENHANCING SOCIAL FUNCTIONING
(Its Place in the Armamentarium of Social Work Treatment Approaches)

As a universal social phenomenon in many cultures and in many human societies, the family can be described in terms of its structure, its functions and its relationship to the larger social system and organization in which it exists.

The family is a social group which usually consists of blood related and/or legally related members who share the place of shelter and other resources for the maintenance of the family members. Usually their social interaction and relationship is on a more intensive level than in other relationships and the group is characterized by interdependence, reciprocity and interaction in a transactional system of which the family is composed. The distribution of social roles, authority and power in the family group depends on the ascribed and assumed roles in the family unit and usually involves intergenerational membership and sub-systems involving both unigenerational and cross-generational relationships. The social role relationships are determined not only by the individual family history, but also by the cultural, social, religious and ethnological composition of the family and by the history of the larger social groupings in which it exists. The social class and ethnic backgrounds of the family members will determine the power structure and whether it is patriarchal, matriarchal, or democratic and egalitarian. Another characteristic of the family group is the fact that it usually is a more permanent grouping. Functionally, also, the family carries major responsibility for the socialization and social control of the individuals composing it. All of these functions are either inadequate or inoperative when family pathology exists. As a social system, the family has to develop methods for coping with its functional responsibilities and problems that arise, and has to maintain a balance in order to meet stress and to reestablish a working basis. The family, as a social system which is an open transactional system, is also related to the culture and social order in which it exists and has to have both form and elasticity in order to meet ever changing needs. The family is composed of sub-systems which are generational such as the spouse system and the sibling system, and intergenerational, such as the parent-child sub-system. The family is responsible for meeting the need satisfactions of the family members to a great extent and provides for the encouragement of growth, maturation, and movement from one life phase to the other of its membership. Also, the family serves as a major medium for developing patterns of communication and provides for the transmission of cultural values. Because of its central function in society, the family is a frequent unit of attention for social work intervention and, of course, is the focus of attention in family counseling.

In working with the family, it is important to determine the goal of family counseling. Family counseling aims at restoring impaired social functioning of a family by supporting current functioning, by strengthening social functioning through the removal of obstacles to the resolution of conflict, by improving division of labor, by facilitating the meeting of basic bio-psycho-social needs of family members, by compensating for deficiencies, and by minimizing excesses. Family counseling is a treatment modality aimed at intervention in a family situation when a family is dysfunctional in any way. The focus of the counselor is on the family as a totality in studying and assessing its functioning, and the intervention is planned on the basis of the needs of the total family and how it affects all of its members.

There is a great deal of difference of opinion in the field of family treatment about whether or not it is essential to intervene in the total family unit at all times in order for this form of counseling to be used, or whether the family counseling modality depends upon the focus of the counselor on the total family situation as the unit of attention for study and determination of the best and most suitable means of intervention.

Generic Criteria for the Use of Family Counseling

Differential criteria for family counseling is based on differential family diagnosis and includes the following: (1) whenever in a family system, stresses or crises create disruption of normal family processes and result in family dysfunction, family counseling would be considered; (2) wherever family members are unable, unwilling, or prevented from carrying out their social roles and therefore disturb the family balance; and (3) wherever the family is unable to use the normal coping mechanisms to deal with interferences in the social functioning of the family. Also, it goes without saying, that the family needs to be in existence in order to utilize the modality of family counseling. The following

9

differential criteria for family treatment need to be considered: (1) social role confusions, ambiguity, distortions, diffusion (not placing responsibility where it belongs); (2) disturbances of family complementarity; (3) individual and family maturational task crises and disturbances of family functioning; (4) inadequate family identity; (5) marital disturbances, parent-child disturbances, sibling relationship dusturbances, extra-familial disturbances, affected by or affecting family functioning; (6) ego defects, for example, character disorders in individual members requiring family participation in treatment; (7) extra-familial disturbances affecting family functioning; (8) other defects and disabling handicaps (physical and social) in individual members requiring family participation; (9) inability or unreadiness to use individual interviews; (10) skill in family diagnosis and treatment on the part of the counselor; (11) family interviewing for diagnostic purposes.

Some contra-indications are: (1) massive unmet dependency and other need satisfactions; (2) chaotic family situations without adequate family identity and depending on the degree of egocentricity of the members of the family; (3) very severe problems of trust and suspiciousness; (4) pathological uses of interrelationship to the detriment of family members such as support of destructive defenses; (5) lack of therapeutic skill on the part of the counselor in this area; (6) absence of a family when the family is already split-up; (7) when an individual finds it too dangerous to function in the family, for example, when one might endanger the welfare of the other members of the family; (8) when the religious, or value system, of a family counter-indicates this approach; (9) when the individual is so needful that he requires individual nurturance in order to be able to function as a member of the family; (10) when the problem is encapsulated in the marriage only; (11) when the individual comes in for information or direction which does not require participation of the family; (12) the lack of skill in dealing with family situations and interaction; (13) the inappropriateness of content dealt with for some members of the family such as the young children.

It can be determined for whom family counseling is indicated in the light of the above stated criteria and contra-indications for family counseling. This treatment modality should be considered in relationship to other modalities such as individual treatment approaches and/or group approaches. The latter refers to artificial, or more temporary groupings such as peer groups, or grouping of individuals and couples, and/or families with common problems, which are used in order to provide the individual client with an opportunity to learn from the group experience other than his natural grouping such as the family.

The family counseling approach requires that the family counselor maintain a family focus in examining situations brought to his attention. On the basis of study and analysis of the problem and assessment of the situation, the family counselor determines the indications for family counseling and/or other treatment modalities and means of intervention.

Footnotes

[1] Counseling (according to Webster's International Dictionary, 2nd edition, 1959) is advice, instruction, especially that given as a result of consultation, interchange of opinions, mutual advising, deliberations together and consultation.

References

Parsons, Talcott, and Robert F. Bales, **Family Socialization and Interaction Process**, Free Press, Glencoe, Illinois, 1955.

Pollak, Otto, "A Family Diagnosis Model," **Social Service Review**, Vol. 34, No. 1, March 1960, pp. 19-31.

Scherz, Frances H., "Multiple-Client Interviewing: Treatment Implications," **Social Casework**, Vol. 43, No. 3, March 1962.

Wynne, Lyman C., Some Indications and Contra-indications for Exploratory Family Therapy." In Ivan Boszormenyi-Nagy and James L. Framo, **Intensive Family Therapy**, Hoeber Medical Division, Harper and Row, New York, 1965, pp. 289-322.

CHAPTER II

HISTORICAL DEVELOPMENT OF
FAMILY COUNSELING

Methods of intervention, diagnosis and treatment in social case work and in counseling owe a great deal to the development of the psychoanalytic movement in the first half of the twentieth century. The consideration of the family in relation to individual behavior and family problems has always been a major focus in social case work, although with the advent of the influence of the psycnoanalytic movement in the 20's and 30's, the family was a secondary unidirectional consideration in terms of how it affected the individual and what needed to be done to change the family in behalf of the individual. As far back as the beginning of the twentieth century, Freud, in his case of little Hans,[1] described a situation in which he worked with the child through the father. In the child guidance movement in the 20's and 30's, in work in behalf of children and also in the work with the mentally ill in mental hospitals, the role of the social worker was largely seen in terms of affecting the physical environment and the social environment of the client, or patient. The family was worked with largely to modify the family situation in behalf of the identified client. Milieu treatment was an outgrowth of these early developments of the continuing effort to affect the milieu of the identified client, or patient, both in terms of the clinical setting, the family and the social environment at large. In direct methods of intervention, in behalf of individuals and families, all the helping disciplines, such as psychiatry, social work, and psychology have been moving since the middle of the century and in the 60's toward more focus on the central role of the family as a very important aspect of the identified client's milieu. There is now a greater conviction that the family needs to be affected per se in order not only to help with the problems presented by the identified, or indexed client, but also in order to help the family which is affected and may be indicating its need for help via the identified client. It is interesting that in all of the helping disciplines, there has been increased emphasis on the family-focused approach, although the emphasis on the individual *per se* is still very strong especially in view of this long-standing emphasis. In the past decade and a half, we have witnessed increasing experimentation in approaching the problems presented by identified clients as seen in their family milieu.

One of the major changes in the conceptual framework underlying family counseling is that instead of focusing mainly on intrapsychic individual functioning and interaction with the counselor, the focus has been moved in family-focused counseling to the transactional system which the family presents and to the social interaction among the family members within the transactional system. The family counselor enters the situation to study and assess family functioning and works in behalf of diminishing and removing dysfunctioning, and/or restoring social functioning of the family. Proponents of the family treatment approach, such as Carl Whitaker and Murray Bowen have stressed the fact that in working in the family situation, it is important that the therapist or the counselor enter into the family transactional system mainly in order to act as a resource for the family in understanding and modifying their functioning and not encouraging undue dependence on the counselor, since this ordinarily leads to regression rather than progression in their functional operations. This does not rule out the need for meeting dependency needs but rather minimizes the undue tendency to strengthen dependency and regression. Research in the field of the family milieu where schizophrenic patients were the identified patients, or clients in the family (such as has been done at Yale University, by the Palo Alto Mental Research Institute, and at the National Research Center at Bethesda, Maryland of the NIMH), have contributed much to current understanding of the role of the family in the interaction of the family with the identified patient, and in the interaction which tends to trigger or enhance the pathological reaction which has been variously termed as schizophrenic behavior. In social work the family focused approach has been the object of particular study. Experimentation has been going on in the development of treatment modalities in this area in such centers as the Palo Alto Mental Research Institute, the Midwest Committee on Family Diagnosis and Treatment of the Family Service Association of America, the Family Mental Health Clinic of the Jewish Family Service of New York City, and in the extensive work of the Community Research Associates in St. Paul, Hennepin County, Minnesota, with the economically indigent, in San Mateo County, California, with the behavior disordered and in Washington County of Maryland with the medically indigent.

Out of the latter has grown the development of the literature on working with multiple problem, hard-to-reach, hard-core families in which the aggressive case work approach was developed early and in which the necessity for working with the total family situation was stressed. In fact, they particularly emphasized the need for an epidemiological approach on a community-wide basis in order to take into account the incidence and prevalence of social dysfunctioning, to identify the affected families and to follow-up with necessary services for families presenting a high degree of social dysfunctioning. (See Alice Voiland, et al., volume on *Family Case Work Diagnosis* as an example of the findings and conclusions of that series of studies; also see other books and articles in the section on family diagnosis and treatment in the bibliographical section.) In social work, the emphasis on the aspect of social functioning of individuals, families, and communities was particularly spelled out in the Social Work Curriculum Study published in 1959 by the Council on Social Work Education (Vols. I through XIV).

The family-centered approach as developed in the studies of families with schizophrenic clients of the NIMH Research Center at Bethesda, Maryland; the Yale University studies which stressed schisms, skews, collusions, and alignments; the Palo Alto Mental Research Institute which stressed the communication approach; the systems theory approach as illustrated in the work of the Midwest Committee in collaboration with Otto Pollak; the emphasis on the transactional theoretical approach as developed by Roy Grinker at the Michael Reese Hospital in Chicago; and in the psychoanalytically centered conflict-resolution approach as developed by Ackerman et. al. at the New York Family Mental Health Institute, all utilized the findings of the social sciences in relation to social role theory. Eric Berne's work on transactional analysis, the influence of ego psychology as exemplified by the writings emanating from Smith College's School of Social Work, e.g., the volumes on *Ego-Oriented Case Work* and *Ego Psychology and Dynamic Case Work*, and the inauguration of the *Journal of Family Process* in March, 1962, all represent the many-faceted developments in this field. All of these developments underline the growing interest in the renewal of effort in behalf of utilizing and modifying the social milieu in which the identified client in his family is operating. They represent the growing utilization of findings and new knowledge from the social sciences in behalf of families and the affected individuals.

Of interest in assessing the place of the family-focused and family-oriented approach is the fact that there has been a change in the place of the family in the therapeutic framework. Namely, there is a growing movement away from looking solely at the family as the source of the pathology, to seeing it as a social organization and system which reflects the adequacy of the social functioning of the system and the individuals comprising it. Rather than seeing treatment as only related to individuals the reciprocal nature of the interactions in the transactional system of the family is emphasized, and, therefore, a more balanced view of the effects of all the interested parties on each other is provided. Thus, we avoid seeing the family interaction as a unidirectional process. This has broadened our perspective and given us greater opportunity for viewing the operation of the family system and the consequences of the interactions of the members of the system, and the nature of the intervention by the counselor. Another effect of the family-focused approach is to minimize the tendency toward victimization, scapegoating and exploitation of the indexed client, or patient, and makes it more likely that the more basic sources of the dysfunctional aspects of the family and individual functioning will be uncovered and addressed. Also the participation of those most directly affected produces a more democratic opportunity for all affected individuals to present their cases and to participate in the resolution of their problems.

As can be seen from the brief sketch outlined above, the family counseling emphasis has been developing rapidly in the past decade and a half, not only in social work but in all other helping disciplines, such as psychiatry, and it represents an attempt to reconcile current social science knowledge with modalities of intervention in behalf of improving the social functioning of families and individuals.

What is becoming increasingly obvious is that the major contribution of the psychoanalytic movement to therapeutic intervention in the functional behavior of individuals as developed by Freud has been focused on utilization of the therapeutic relationship as a means for projecting the individual's patterns of responding and communicating and behaving onto the therapist in a therapeutically neutral environment. He was helped in this relationship to become more aware of these response patterns and through the therapeutic intervention to relearn and recondition the patient to more adaptive modes of response. The family treatment and family counseling approach moves a step further in the light of modern social science theory and knowledge to utilize what we know about family interaction and operations to maximize the utilization of the family situation, where indicated, for diagnostic and therapeutic purposes. Hence, the normal, or the usual family milieu, in which individuals have their major socialization needs met, have social provisions made, and have their need satisfactions met to a major extent, is utilized both for purposes of understanding the nature of the dysfunction, and also for correcting the dysfunction at one of its central points of origin and operation. Insofar as this is feasible, the family counseling approach is indicated and appears to be a promising area for further development in the helping professions' efforts to assist individuals and families.

1. Freud, S., "Analysis of a Phobia in a Five Year Old Boy", **Collected Papers**, Vol. 3, London, Hogarth Press, 1949, pp. 149-289.

References

Ackerman, Nathan W., "A Dynamic Frame for the Clinical Approach to Family Conflict," **Exploring the Base for Family Therapy**, eds. Nathan W. Ackerman, F. L. Beatman, and S. N. Sherman, New York, Family Service Association of America, 1961.

Ackerman, Nathan W., Frances L. Beatman, and Sanford N. Sherman, eds., **Exploring the Base for Family Therapy**, Family Service Association of America, New York, 1961.

Ackerman, Nathan W., Frances L. Beatman, and Sanford N. Sherman, eds., **Expanding Theory and Practice in Family Therapy**, Family Service Association of America, New York, 1967.

Bardill, Donald R., and Francis J. Ryan, **Family Group Casework**, Catholic University of America Press, Washington, D. C., 1964.

Berne, Eric, **Transactional Analysis in Psychotherapy**, New York, Grove Press, 1961.

Boehm, Werner, **Social Work Curriculum Study** Council on Social Work Education, New York, 1959.

Boszormenyi-Nagy, Ivan, M.D., and James L. Framo, Ph.D., eds., **Intensive Family Therapy**, New York, Harper and Row, Hoeber Medical Division, 1965, Chapter 5.

Bowen, Murray, The Use of Family Theory in Clinical Practice, **Comprehensive Psychiatry** Vol. 7, No. 5, October 1966, pp. 345-374.

Bowen, Murray, "The Family as the Unit of Study and Treatment Workshop, 1959. I. Family Psychotherapy," **American Journal of Orthopsychiatry**, XXXI, January 1961.

Flugel, J. D., **The Psychoanalytic Study of the Family**, London, Hogarth Press, 1921.

Grinker, Roy S., **Psychiatric Social Work: A Transactional Case Book**, New York, Basic Books, Inc., 1961.

Lidz, Theodore, Stephen Fleck and Alice Cornelison, **Schizophrenia and the Family**, International University Press, New York, 1966.

Lidz, Theodore, M.D., **The Family and Human Adaptation**l New York, International Universities Press, Inc., 1963.

Parad, Howard I., **Ego Psychology and Dynamic Casework**, Family Service Association of America, 1958.

Parad, Howard I., and Roger R. Miller, **Ego-Oriented Casework**, Family Service Association of America, New York, 1963.

Parsons, Talcott, "The American Family: Its Relation to Personality and to Social Structure," **The Family Socialization and Interaction Process**, eds., Talcott Parsons, R. F. Ball, Glencoe, Illinois, Free Press of Glencoe, Illinois, 1955.

Pollak, Otto, and Donald Brieland, "The Midwest Seminar in Family Diagnosis and Treatment," **Social Casework**, Vol. 42, No. 7, July 1961, p. 319.

Casebook on Family Diagnosis and Treatment, Family Service Association of America, New York, 1964.

Satir, Virginia, **Conjoint Family Therapy**, Science and Behavior Books, Inc., Palo Alto, California, 1968.

Voiland, Alice L. and Associates, **Family Casework Diagnosis**, New York and London, Columbia University Press, 1962.

Wynne, Lyman, "The Study of Intrafamilial Alignments and Splits in Exploratory Family Therapy," **Exploring the Base for Family Therapy**, eds., Nathan W. Ackerman, F. L. Beatman and S. N. Sherman, New York, Family Service Association of America, 1961.

CHAPTER III

THEORETICAL UNDERPINNINGS,
SCHOOLS OF THOUGHT,
SEMANTICS AND TERMINOLOGIES

Theoretical Underpinnings for an Eclectic
Approach to Family Counseling

The well established concepts and principles which form the foundation of practice of counseling and social case work, also apply to family counseling and serve as the basis for the further development of a family-focused approach. The frame of reference used is the social case work approach to counseling with the additional application of family theory as it is at present being developed in the social sciences, and adapted to the field of family counseling. The centers for such development have already been mentioned previously and we will be discussing further at this point their place in the currently established framework underpinning family counseling practice. The theoretical contributions emanating from these centers need to be correlated and compared, and practice will determine their validity and applicability.

The theoretical framework upon which the individual approach in counseling in social case work has been developed includes, of course, heavy emphasis and reliance on psychoanalytic theory with its focus on the psychobiological approach to behavior, with special reference to the psychosexual stages of development as described by Freud and his followers. Also the stages of development were further elaborated by Erik Erikson. More recently emphasis has been placed on ego psychological functional aspects of behavior. The emphasis has moved in counseling and social case work to the latter in recent decades. The preoccupation with the unconscious aspects of the personality and the sources of behavior have remained an area of special competence of psychoanalytic practitioners, psychologists, and others who have access through their methods of exploration and intervention and who can attempt to work on that level. In counseling, however, the focus is more on the conscious aspects of the functioning of the personality and of behavior. The goal is to affect behavior through expanding self-awareness and hence greater ability of the individual to cope with his conscious behavior more adequately.

In shifting the focus from the individual *per se* to the individual in his situation as in family counseling where we lay stress on the individual in his family setting as the major focus, we need to bring in theoretical underpinnings from the social sciences to help us understand the family (its composition, the dynamics operating in the family as a transactional system, its contribution to the individual's functioning, and vice versa the individual's contribution to the family's operations). We have also come to the thought where there is growing agreement that in order to understand the family it is important to see it in actual operation and to observe, and where appropriate, to intervene in its operations in order to make the contribution of the family counselor most effective. Hence, this treatment modality involves direct work with the family as a group. This requires the use of knowledge and skills in observing and studying, analyzing, assessing and planning appropriate interventions for such family situations.

A Structural-Functional Approach to the Family

In order to understand the family and its operations, the concepts borrowed from systems theory are useful insofar as it helps us to have an appropriate method of approach to the family in structural as well as in operational terms. Hence, in approaching a family situation, we need to view it in the light of its specific structure and what this contributes to its functioning. Also from systems theory we utilize the concept that in each system there is an input which is fed into the system in terms of the contributions of the individuals which make up a family. Then there are the interactional processes that take place in the transactional system of the family in its outcome, or output. In relation to input, this would be the use of resources, what is available, what the system does with it, in to what it is converted, and finally, what the outcomes are in terms of output. The system is also affected by feedback, both within the system and also in its relationship with other systems, which involves processes of communication, reciprocal action and feeding in of information. Then we need to determine how the system copes with the situation, how its balance is affected and what happens in the course of its rebalancing as there are effects from these inputs. This feedback could be of a corrective nature which may either increase deviation, counteract it, or reduce it; or lead to defensive reactions like reaction-formation over-compensation; or it may reinforce individual ways of behaving, such as turning to oneself rather than interacting. This may bring about feelings of rejection and lack of need satisfaction which cause further deviance in the operations of the system. It is the counselor's job to understand these processes, to utilize his entry into the system and to intervene in appropriate fashion.

Often the first visible signs of what is going on in the system are in relation to the output of the system where we first come in touch with the family and its methods of operation. We need to move from the output back into the operations within the family and begin to see if we can effect the input and the process going on which results in the output. Our task is not only to improve the input but also the communications system, the transactions and the feedback in order to diminish, or change, the non-adaptive modes of operation of the family as a group.

We look at the family as a system, a social organization of either blood, or legally related, or socially related individuals who are interacting, who share a system of values, who are interdependent, who have a more intense form of emotional relationship and usually there is some sharing of resources, shelter and means of survival. The system makes it possible for certain operational processes to take place which are related to the functioning of the system which also has boundaries and a certain defined structure. In the simplest definition [1] a system is a set of objects together with relationships between the objects and between their attributes. When we are describing the family counseling process, we are focusing largely on the nuclear family and its operations. Therefore, in using a systems approach towards understanding the nuclear family, the model, to which we shall address ourselves, will be largely confined to the nuclear family.

Focusing on the nuclear family, we would refer to a model such as that suggested by Otto Pollak [2] in which he posited the model for the American nuclear family of the average, or the ideal family consisting of two parents, and the children not too far removed in age from each other to avoid interference with their being in the same generation. This may be used as a base by which to judge, for example, structural normality, or deviance, excesses in structure, deficits in structure. Also we need to think of the possible sub-systems that exist within such a model, such as the spouse system, the parent-child system and the sibling system. We need to judge the developmental and maturational level of the family and its membership. It is important to determine how the behavior of the individual in the family affects that of others according to the principle of pervasiveness of family disturbance which Murray Bowen speaks of as the "undifferentiated ego mass" of the family. Redl and others speak of this process as contagion. The principle of indeterminacy refers to the fact that the output of a family system will depend on not only the input, but also the maturational level, and the structure of the family, as to how it affects its coping ability and its equilibrium, what new equilibrium needs to be established in order to cope with changes in equilibrium caused by the input, and the process going on within the family situation and the system which affects the output. Then by feedback mechanisms we may learn how the family is affected by other systems with which it interacts and within which it operates, such as the extended family, the neighborhood, the sub-cultural grouping, the ethnic or religious grouping, the value system, and the social class of the family.

Transactional theory refers to the system, for example, the family, as a set of interrelationships which affect each other mutually in a systematic fashion; the inter-actional aspects of the system refer to the effect of one of the members on the other, as they affect each other mutually. The whole situation comprises the transactional aspects of the system.

Field theory stresses the environmental influences on the two person system, for example, of worker and client. The field is the matrix surrounding, or the environ-ment as a constantly changing and powerful influence.

Communication consists of verbal and non-verbal mes-sages which are received, acknowledged and corrected in cyclical transactions which change in time and by virtue of communication feedbacks; learning occurs for both. Role performances are represented by communica-tions within the transactional system. They have ex-plicit and implicit meanings with past learning and identification and current relearnings. On this basis mutual understanding occurs. Transference and counter-transference are used to indicate the nature of com-munications and the emotional effects of both participants on each other in the transactional system.

Communication theory involves both verbal and non-verbal behavior within the social context, or interaction, or transaction. It includes symbols and clues used by persons in giving and receiving meanings which are reliable indicators of interpersonal functioning. As we observe and study, we see the relationship of patterns in communication and systematic behavior. We need clarity to communicate information to others and to see ourselves and others. We need to label things properly by the use of semantic connotations, words, and ex-periences that they can expect. We need to learn about relationships by asking and responding. Words can have different meanings such as denotations and they can have different connotations, that is, implications of a word like "mother." Words are symbols and may stand for different things and are used at different levels of abstraction.

Words are tools for giving and getting information, for sharing feelings, for perceptions, for evaluations of alternatives and for anthropomorphic allusions.

Often we assume falsely that we can be in another's skin, and know how they think and feel, or that others know this about us. We each ask for clarification by each to be sure about the meaning. Are the communicators functional or dysfunctional? Are they helpful or hindering understanding and communication?

Functional communication requires firm statements of the case, clarity, feedback and receptiveness to feedback. Both communicators are responsible for this. Generalizations without feedback are dangerous. Dysfunctional people are not aware of these needs and act accordingly by sending incomplete and confused messages, or conflicting doublebind messages. They do not make connections and they give incomplete messages which leaves the person to whom the communication is directed uncertain about what is meant. Incomplete messages may be like code or shorthand. It could be a way of easy communication among those who are already in good communication but can be a source of confusion to those who are not. It also can be used in the service of dysfunctional behavior which results in conflict, aggression, destructiveness, etc. Non-verbal communication by gestures of the face and other parts of the body, by posture, tone, voice and dress are also other sources of messages. We may communicate on a denotative level giving meaning, on a metacommunicative level commenting on the literal content as well as on the nature of the persons involved, or a message about a message like threatening gestures. The person may give such communication more meaning by labeling it. People ask for the purpose, make requests and give warnings, in giving metacommunications, and receive certain implications from them.

In the functional family it is necessary for each to help the other understand the communication. The degree of freedom in communicating determines the effectiveness of the communication.

Messages can be congruent and fit, or be incongruent. More than one message often can be contradictory in their implications. Congruent messages are in context. Incongruent messages are on different levels of communication and may be more or less conflicting. Messages involve a sender and a receiver, a message and a context and may be given in the form of a request. In order to understand the communication, interaction must be observed to determine whether the messages and communications are functional or dysfunctional for the situation and the context; e.g., man needs to accept difference and ambivalence to free himself for creative living.

Small group theory stresses that in moving from the concentration on the intrapsychic aspects of the individual's adjustment and behavior to his functioning in his situation in his family setting, we have to think of the fit between the behavior of the individual and the family situation which has been compared to that of a mold and a template. The family system resists change. This is the basis for the balance, or equilibrium, or dynamic steady state. Homeostasis is the characteristic of systems that enables them, when disturbed, to counteract disturbance, and to return to their previous balance. It is a constantly changing process depending on the circumstances under which the system is operating. The amount of change possible within this system of balance determines the flexibility of the family, for example, and it's range and repertoire of response to change. In the GAP Report on "Integration and Conflict in Family Behavior," Report #27—there is a statement by Florence Kluckhohn and John P. Spiegel which suggested five foci around which knowledge about the family needs to be developed, namely, the individual, the group, the social system, the cultural values, and the geographic location. All of these factors interpenetrate and interact with each other. Mary Louise Somers[3] stated that the group approach to family health problems has made the point that it is important in understanding families via the diagnostic process to utilize the systems approach, seeing the family as the system. She describes the use of an intersystems model which deals with the nuclear and the extended family relationship, as well as a developmental model which contains reference to the maturational growth model for individual families which in turn includes growth, change, development and dissolution.

In terms of the family group processes that are involved, Grace L. Coyle[4] states that in defining the family as a small group, we need to use seven processes from small group theory that are relevant to determining the social functioning, or dysfunctioning of the family, namely:

1. Group formation of the family, including deter-

mination of its membership and the formulation of individual and family group goals.

2. The development of family group structure both formal and informal.
3. Development of interpersonal relationships and patterns and development of leadership and followership within the family.
4. Development of group controls and the exercise and distribution of authority among family members and among various family roles.
5. Development of communication, deliberation, and decision-making within the problem-solving process essential for day-to-day living for handling family conflicts and for action as a group.
6. Development of family group cohesion and morale.
7. Development of family group norms and values.

These are the bases for the determination of family identity and group development. Mary Louise Somers points out that in understanding the formation of a family group, it is important to know on what basis the spouses selected each other to form the family, what is the legal basis of the family, who was responsible for support and nurturing in the socialization process and for the maturation of the children.

Attention has to be given to group goals of the family, for very often part of the help given to the family consists of enabling them to become clearer about their goals and to make them functional. It also may mean helping them to develop processes of communication, of deliberation, of decision making, of development of mutually accepted goals, of development of group cohesion and morale which in turn is based on personal and family group identity (which are reciprocally inter-dependent). The family group identity, according to Erik Erikson, is the matrix in which the individual's ego identity is developed based on one's sameness and differentness in the family and the continuity of the family members intergenerationally and generationally. How one affects the group may be accomplished through affecting individuals within the group, and also the group as a whole. Change in either brings about change in all involved. It is important to identify the particular patterns of each family, its pattern of equilibrium, how it maintains its cohesion and balance, what is the role performance of its members and the value system under which it is operating (which determines how flexible or rigid the family's control mechanisms are). In working with the family as a group, the most productive base for effective intervention is the maintenance of a focus on the interaction between the parts of the family's system rather than on the internalized conflict of its members.

In considering the family as a group, one naturally focuses on the interaction of the family members which can be seen from the point of view of their social roles. These roles are either ascribed to the individual by virtue of his position in the family, or assumed by virtue of his role performance. The specific structure of the family, the opportunities it offers for such role assumption, and the interaction among all the members of the family present us with the role network in the family. Our focus should be on the interaction of these roles and the functional and dysfunctional aspects of their performance. One can analyze and study the family system by assessing the social roles of the family members and the effectiveness with which they are carried out by the members of the family group. The nature of the family system determines how roles are carried out, and the opportunity the individual has for clarity, ease or strain, ambiguity, discontinuity, diffusion, and confusion of his social roles and their performance. The expectations and the perceptions of these roles may be congruent or incongruent, and, therefore, either contribute or not to their functionality. The individual adaptation and potentials of the members of the family determine the role performance. Social role theory helps in understanding the social dynamics and determinants of behavior. How the individual is affected by a social group like the family is reflected in the way he functions as an individual, his adjustment to reality, and the effectiveness of the ego aspects of his personality in carrying out their executive functions in mediating in mediating between the drive life of the individual and the realities of the external world. This is basic for the development of the control mechanism, or the super-ego, according to psychoanalytic theory.

Socio-behavioral theory has highlighted concepts from learning theory which need to be integrated into our practice and should also be related to family counseling, for example, the importance of specifying problematic behavior, and why these behaviors tend to recur. What are the stimuli which reinforce them? The theory emphasizes that whether behavior is considered adaptive, mal-adaptive, deviant or normal, depends upon the interpretation of the person who is exhibiting the behavior and the observer.

In socio-behavioral theory, it is important to determine the condition which creates the problematic behavior. The theory refers particularly to the external factors such as: familial handling of behavior, peer reference groups, delinquent groups and expectations in group living situations. Also included is the indication of the desired behavior which the therapist attempts to inculcate in the client. There has to be an identification of the exact techniques to be used, and the short term and long term goals which need to be addressed. Richard B. Stuart[5] stresses three basic assumptions in the socio-behavioral approach to casework:

1. All social behavior is learned and can be modified through the application of the principles of learning.
2. All psychotherapies involve a teaching and learning experience.
3. A more deliberate application of our knowledge of the learning process to psychotherapy would yield far more effective results.

He stresses that the determination of the goals to be achieved are part of the therapeutic contract. The therapist is the client's agent, treating only what is specifically determined jointly by the client and the therapist, so that the goals are the product of mutual assent. They are explicit. They are amenable to periodic monitoring by both the client and the worker. The attitude of mutuality assures commitment to goal attainment by the client and by the therapist. Explicitness creates the condition necessary for precise treatment planning. Monitor-ability allows both the client and the therapist to have information about the effectiveness of their efforts to indicate whether changes in the plan are necessary. The theory also stresses the importance of relationships which makes the treatment situation attractive to the client and increases his willingness to participate. It emphasizes that the "milieu" in which the client exists determines the adaptiveness of his behavior, and that behavior is the individual's response to internal and external stimuli, so that behavior might be the result of inappropriate stimulus control.

For psychosomatic illnesses, for example, we have a lack of stimulus control, where the stimulus does not bring about the expected response, and the individual's reinforcing system does not help him to develop such controls. There might be inappropriate reinforcement of inappropriate behavior. In this approach, behavioral assessment is equivalent to diagnosis in the regular treatment process. It collects data about the problem— relevant behavior and responses, and seeks to identify the stimulus conditions under which the responses occur and can be expected to be modified. One has to identify the eliciting stimuli to determine the conditions under which the problematic operant behavior occurs. One must then identify the discriminative and the reinforcing stimulus. Conditions need to be created which extinguish the non-adaptive response through desensitizing and corrective experiences which then extinguish the original response such as anxiety or fear, and make the behavior more adaptive. This theory states that behavioral changes can be understood as the process of altering responses to existing stimuli so that one can alter responses to existing forces to change the environment, and thus alter both his responses and his environment. Florence Hollis[6] comments that she believes the Gestalt Theory emphasizing comprehension, understanding, and insight, rather than positive or negative reinforcement (reward and punishment), is more akin and relevant to social case work as developed at the present time. The Gestalt Theory takes into account the client's own choice. Florence Hollis stresses the fact that a greater degree of self-

determination is characteristic of the Gestalt psychol-
ogies and, therefore, is more consonant with the emphasis
on giving the client the major control over his own
treatment. Miss Hollis does not deny the possible appropriate use of operant conditioning and the use of socio-
behavioral theory when specified in mutually agreed
upon areas of work with clients.

Semantics and Terminology

In order to clarify the use of terms and our frame
of reference, we are offering the following definitions
of frequently used terms in this section:

Family counseling as contrasted with individual counseling is oriented toward viewing family functioning and
its effect on the individual, and reciprocally the effect
of the individual on the family in contrast to the individual-centered approach which focuses on the functioning and the dynamics of the individual *per se.*

Family-focused counseling approach refers to the fact
that the unit of attention in this approach is the family
and its social functioning.[7]   In the family-focused approach the emphasis is on the aspects of mutuality,
**reciprocity, complementarity, communication, role net-
work** and the structure and function of the family as a
system.

Family diagnosis and treatment refers to the family-
focused approach in both the study and treatment phases.
Though it does not imply necessarily sole attention to
the family as a unit, it does imply that at some point
it is desirable to observe the family as a unit in its
functioning in order to understand the dynamics of the

family and its problems. The treatment method does not necessarily need to concentrate only on work with the family unit. It may entail a combination of family unit, multiple interview, conjoint treatment of the spouses. Pairs and other segments of the family may be seen separately as indicated. An individual treatment approach may be used as needed.

The family is a social system. In viewing the family as an open-ended system which grows and develops, expands and contracts in the course of its existence, it needs to be examined both structually and on an intergenerational basis and on a peer basis, for example, the classification as suggested by Otto Pollak including the spouse system, the parent-child sub-system, and the sibling sub-system.

In discussing the *counseling process*, we used the *method* to refer to the total counseling activity. When we use the term *process* we refer to the specifics of the counseling process such as the interactions between counselor and client, among clients, and among the clients and the counselor.

The terms *transaction* and *interaction* refer to the fact that any communication, or behavioral interchange, between two or more individuals is an interaction and the reciprocal interaction between two or more individuals is the transaction, or the transactional system going on between, or among, them.

An Eclectic Approach to Family Treatment

As we indicated earlier, an eclectic approach in family counseling involves the use of multiple theoretical formulations and frameworks about human behavior and about the functioning of the family as an open, evolving system which is constantly shifting in its balance and equilibrium in order to adapt itself to its current circumstances. In order to understand the family system with which we are confronted in the counseling situation, it is important to understand the total system as well as its component parts. This requires the use of knowledge from a variety of theories to which we previously referred in order to understand the dynamics operating within its component parts. If we view the system as a dynamic living social configuration in which on-going transactional processes take place, we need to observe the interactions of which the transactional system is comprised and how it is functioning. This requires observation not only of the interactions but also some observation of knowledge of the individuals in the family. Such information can be gathered from observation of the family in the process of its functioning, as well as from gathering of data about the family indirectly and collaterally where indicated or necessary. The counselor, since he works with the conscious parts of the individual's functioning, focuses on the capacities, the coping abilities and the resources, sometimes referred to as strengths of the individuals who compose the family system, and also on the resources and strengths of the family as a system.

Small group theory is helpful in understanding the structure of the family as a system insofar as we utilize knowledge about the composition, formation, power structure, membership, lines of authority, decision-making processes, assignment of roles and communication systems operating in the family system. In addition, the physical environment and resources of the family, the stage of the family's development, its maturational level, its assets and liabilities, deficits and excesses, and the operational maintenance of equilibrium of the family as a system are taken into account. We also consider the goals of the family as a system, its value system, the need-response patterns and need satisfactions such as handling of aggressive, affectional and sexual needs and its effect on the growth and development of its individual members. Also, we take into account both the functional and dysfunctional aspects of the individual functioning of the family members, in order to assess the functional capacity and efficiency of the family system and to identify areas of dysfunctioning which require intervention. For example, where the identified client is a child presenting behavior difficulties, we need not only to understand the child and its functioning but also the interaction of the child *with* the other family members to determine the reciprocal relationships and effects. Or, in a marital situation, again, we need to determine whether the problem is focused solely in the marital relationship, or whether it is a reflection of the transactional system in the family and how it is operating.

The methods of intervention and treatment of the situation are determined by the structural aspects (deficits and excesses). Do these require attention? Can they be modified? Do they need to be taken into account? Also we need to determine the functional aspects which should be the foci of attention. For example, are there deficits in the family such as the absence of a parent? What is the shift in roles? What compensations need to be built into the family situation in order to substitute for the deficits and to maintain a more adequate family equilibrium? Where there are dysfunctional aspects such as delinquent behavior, under-achievement, or job maladjustment, we need to determine whether the problem resides mainly within the individual and the external circumstances, and how it is affected by and affects the family system. Is John's underachievement in school due primarily to organic deficits or dysfunction, or is it affected by external circumstances in school and at home, or by both? If there are difficulties in meeting maturational growth tasks, it may be a matter of introducing information that is lacking, giving guidance and educational assistance, or it may be a matter of demonstrating in the family situation how this could be handled and improved. Is Mary's immaturity and lack of frustration tolerance in the classroom and with her peers socially due to social disorganization in the family or school, or neighborhood, or neurotic overprotection at home, or maturational gaps in her development, or a combination of factors? If the problem is within the individuals involved, how can this be affected through the family system where perhaps it needs to be dealt with more directly in terms of the individual's own situation? Different sub-systems in the family system may be affected and these may have to be dealt with individually as well as in relation to the total family configuration.

Footnotes

[1] "A Survey of General Systems Theory", by O. R. Young, **General Systems**, Vol. 9, 1964, p. 66.

[2] **Social Service Review**, March 1960, Vol. 34, No. 1, pp. 19-31.

[3] "Group Process Within the Family Unite" Monograph VII, **Social Work Practice in Medical Care and Rehabilitation Settings**, NASW, 1965.

"Concepts Relevant to Helping the Family as a Group", **Social Casework**, Vol. 43, No. 7, July 1962, pp. 347-354.

Footnotes - Cont'd

⁵ "Applications of Behavior Theory to Social Casework." **Socio-Behavioral Approach and Applications to Social Work,** pp. 19-20.

⁶ "And What Shall we Teach?" The Social Work Educator and Knowledge, **Social Service Review,** Vol. 42, No. 2, pp. 84-196, June 1968.

⁷ In this document we will be using the terms "family counseling" and "family-focused casework" interchangeably and synonymously.

References

Bardill, Donald R., and Francis J. Ryan, **Family Group Casework: A Casework Approach to Family Therapy,** Catholic University of America Press, Washington, D. C., 1964.

Berne, Eric, **Transactional Analysis in Psychotherapy,** Grove Press, New York, 1961.

Boszormenyi-Nagy, Ivan, M.D., and James L. Frame, Ph.D., eds., **Intensive Family Therapy,** Harper and Row, Hoeber Medical Division, New York, 1965.

Erikson, Erik H., **Childhood and Society,** W. W. Norton and Company, New York, 1963.

Erikson, Erik H., "The Problem of Ego Identity," in **Psychological Issues,** Vol. I, Part 1, Identity and the Life Cycle, New York, International Universities Press, 1959.

Family Service Association of America, **Casebook on Family Diagnosis and Treatment,** New York, 1964.

Grinker, Roy S., **Psychiatric Social Work: A Transactional Case Book,** Basic Books, Inc., New York, 1961.

Hollis, Florence, ".....And What Shall We Teach?" **Social Service Review,** Vol. 42, No. 2, June 1968, pp. 184-196.

Miller, James G., "Living Systems: Basic Concepts," **Behavorial Science,** Vol. 10, No.3, July 1965, pp. 193-237.

Miller, James G., "Living Systems: Structure and Process," **Behavorial Science,** Vol. 10, No. 4, October 1965, pp. 337-379.

Miller, James G., "Living Systems: Cross-Level Hypotheses" **Behavorial Science,** Vol. 10, No. 4, October 1965, pp. 380-411.

National Association of Social Workers, ed., **The Family is the Patient,** Monograph VII in the series "Social Work Practice in Medical Care and Rehabilitation Settings," New York, 1965.

Ruesch, Jurgen, **Disturbed Communication,** New York, W. W. Norton and Company, 1958.

Ruesch, Jurgen, **Therapeutic Communication,** W. W. Norton and Company, New York, 1961.

Satir, Virginia, **Conjoint Family Therapy,** Science and Behavior Books, Inc., Palo Alto, California, 1968.

Stuart, Richard B., "Applications of Behavior Theory to Social Casework," in Edwin J. Thomas, **Socio-Behavioral Approach and Applications to Social Work,** Council on Social Work Education, New York, 1967, pp. 19-20.

Watzlawick, P., **An Anthology of Human Communication,** Science and Behavior Books, Inc., Palo Alto, California, 1963.

CHAPTER IV

APPLICATION TO SOCIAL
CASE WORK PRACTICE

Generic Application of Family Diagnostic
and Treatment Approaches to the Fields
of Social Case Work Practice

We start with the definition of social case work practice or counseling practice as a method of rehabilitative intervention when individuals and families cannot cope with their life tasks. This may occur because of difficulties within themselves, difficulties in the family, or difficulties in meeting the demands of social and institutional forces in their environment.

Social case work, or family counseling is a method of intervention for purposes of helping to correct imbalances existing between the individual's or the family's capacity for meeting internal needs and the demands of their environment. These imbalances are reflected in terms of personal and social dysfunctioning and maladaptation. The aim is to bring about a new balance so that the individuals involved may be free to utilize their capacities and their opportunities in order to cope effectively with their life tasks and situations and continue in their growth and development.

In establishing the aims of a counseling process, it is very important that the counselor and the clients achieve mutually agreed upon goals for their joint endeavors. These goals are subject to constant redefinition during the process of counseling, but must always entail a high degree of mutuality since the focus should remain on the needs of the client. The goals need to be related to the clients' on-going needs and readiness to use such a process. Therefore, goals which are unilaterally determined, either by client, or by the counselor, are usually insufficient in order to be effective. In addition, insofar as the counselor is able to enlist the client's participation in the determination and achievement of mutually agreed upon goals, he is furthering the client's growing ability to cope with this situation and solve the problems which have brought him into the counseling situation.

The problems brought to the attention of the counselor are focused on a variety of areas and very often depend not only on the location of the problem in the client's situation, but also may be related to the institutional setting in which the problem is identified. Yet, even though the point of entry into the situation may differ, the focus in general may be the same; namely, we need to assess the client's environmental situation beginning with the familial situation. Proceeding from there we decide whether the point of entry would include the total family.

In some settings such as the school, for example, the focus is on the learner and the problem for which the learner is referred may appear to be centered in him. However, when it is a problem involving social dysfunctioning, we need to look at more than the identified client in order to determine its relationship to significant individuals in his environment including the family and others in his learning situation. For example, in discussing underachievement it may be related to the attitude a teacher may have toward a particular child, or, on the other hand, it may be related to the family attitudes towards learning which on the surface may be one of which they may not be conscious.

In some settings such as the school, for example, the focus is on the learner and the problem for which the learner is referred may appear to be centered in him. However, when it is a problem involving social dysfunctioning, we need to look at more than the identified client in order to determine its relationship to significant individuals in his environment including the family and others in his learning situation. For example, in discussing underachievement it may be related to the attitude a teacher may have toward a particular child, or, on the other hand, it may be related to the family attitudes towards learning which on the surface may be one of which they may not be conscious.

To be more specific, when a nine year old child was referred to the school social worker because of underachievement, it was found that the teacher had identified him with a relative of hers who had difficulties in learning. Still in another situation, when an eleven year old boy was referred for underachievement, it was found that this was not related to the lack of capacity on his part as much as it was to the family behavioral patterns where the boy was fearful of any competition with his own father in terms of achieving.

In family and marriage counseling settings, the problem frequently is presented in relation to one of the individuals in the family or among some of the individuals. Though we continue to follow the old principle established by Mary Richmond of starting where the client is, we need to determine whether that is the most important problem which needs resolution. In family counseling we are obviously focused on the interaction among the individuals in the situation. Unless it is determined that the problem resides mainly within an individual and the only way of resolving the issue is to help the client resolve his internalized difficulties, we need to examine his interactions with significant people within his environment, especially in the family. We need to determine whether the point of intervention should remain as specified in the initial request, or whether we need to help the client see his relationship to the others and how his problems of malfunctioning are related to his participation in whatever transactional systems he is significantly involved. In family counseling also, as indicated earlier, we need to look at the sub-systems in the family and determine whether the focus should be on one of the sub-systems such as the spouse relationship, which would bring the focus onto the marital situation, or whether it would be among the other sub-systems.

For example, a family is referred for family counseling because the problem appears to be in the sexual relationship of the couple and in the reported impotence in the man. Upon review of the immediate situation, it becomes apparent that although this has been a problem recently, it is related to the presence of one of the spouses' parents. Later it became evident that this was not the only focus of the problem but also that there were difficulties in relation to one of the children in the family who was the initial focus of attention in the school situation. After the intergenerational problem was resolved by the in-law's removal from the family, the focus then moved on to the relationships among the parents and all the children who now were brought into the treatment situation.

Thus, we see an example of a tendency to move from one member of the family to the other as the focus of attention of the problems. After the focus is placed on the interaction among the members of the family, we begin to become increasingly aware of the contribution of each member of the family, and of the individual problems with which each member of the family is coping. As all the members of the family learn to communicate better and to understand each others' feelings about themselves and each other, the tensions in the family are reduced. Each is helped to resolve his own problems and also to become more cooperative in working on the family's problem of functioning more comfortably.

Finally, agreement about how to utilize the family's resources such as the TV, agreement on church affiliation and attendance, agreement on participation in and accomplishment of chores and in greater respect for each other's comfort in terms of not interfering with each other's activities, being sensitive to need for quiet at certain periods and sharing of facilities indicates a new balance has been established.

Another example is that of a child welfare setting which provides substitute care for children where the young mother, who separated from her husband, came to apply for institutional placement for two latency aged boys because of her inability to "control their behavior" and school underachievement. As the worker began to assess the situation, she recognized that the mother's inability to exercise any limits on the children's behavior was due to the fact that she was actually relinquishing her role and was giving it to one of the older boys in the family, who in turn was resented by the two younger boys in question. As the worker continued to see the entire family, this became clear to the mother, who indicated that this was the first time she recognized what was happening and the kind of interaction that took place in the family situation. She was able, with encouragement and support from the worker, gradually to assume more responsibility for limit setting and more constructive disciplining of the children, which then enabled the two boys to remain within the family and improve their adjustment.

In a setting serving aging persons, there was great difficulty determining whether or not the mother of the man could remain in his home, or whether it would be preferable for her to enter a home for the aged. There was a great deal of confusion in the application process in determining whether or not the mother was willing and needed to come in at this point, with the husband and wife having a great deal of difference about the way in which they interpreted the need and readiness for the mother to come into the home. When the three individuals were finally brought in for a multiple family-centered interview, to discuss the aging mother's situation, it became apparent that although she had some hesitancy, actually she was not comfortable in the son's home. In the home of the son, there were younger adolescent children who had very noisy activites which were difficult for the grandmother to tolerate. The son, on the other hand, had some feeling that if the mother were placed, it would be a reflectin on him. It meant to him that he was not giving adequate care to his mother who now needed some supervision because of failing faculties, although she was still partially able to care for herself. She had been employed until very recently in her occupation even though she was well along in her seventies. The daughter-in-law had not been able to make clear the reason why she felt the mother would be happier in a home for the aging. It was not until all three met together and the mother was asked directly that she was able to express what her feelings were and what her situation was, so that the son was no longer unclear about his mother's intention. Also clarified was the economic situation which was complicated because there was some contribution being made by the aging person, there also would be sufficient funds available for placement which the aging person apparently preferred at this point. After clarifying the situation in one interview, the placement was effected with immediate diminution of the stress created by the difficulty in reaching this decision. With the relief of guilt about this decision it was possible for each to undertake the change in living arrangement with sufficient comfort and ease.

ISSUES IN FAMILY COUNSELING

The Eclectic Versus a Unidimensional Theoretical Approach

In presenting an eclectic approach to family counseling, we make reference to the many points of view which we have described above contributing to this theoretical framework. This involves utilizing a great variety of theoretical sources in relation to our understanding of human growth and development, the effect of the social environ ent, and the physical, biological and economic situation of the individual which was described earlier. In terms of the way in which people function individually and in interaction with each other, we need to draw upon the different schools of thought in the social sciences such as social psychology, sociology, anthropology, economics, political science, etc. Then, in addition, we need to consider the philosophy of counseling being utilized.

For example, if the focus of the counseling process is

on the social interaction of the clientele, then it is important to take into account a multi-directional process which flows from counselor to client, from client to client, and from the clients to the counselor. Hence, one has to take into account the communications, the feedbacks, and the operations of the system as a whole which is the focus of attention. In earlier models of counseling which were based on the medical model where the focus was on the individual and what is dysfunctional within him, the focus in such a process was mainly on finding out what the deviation was in the individual and correcting it within the individual. However, in the family counseling focus, it is important not only to pay attention to what is dysfunctional within the individual but also to what is dysfunctional among individuals. Therefore, one has to study the individuals plus their operations with each other so that the social processes become an important object of our attention.

Since our major focus is on social functioning, it is understandable that the counseling process depends upon study, evaluation and assessment of the social processes taking place in the social interaction among the individuals within the family situation and the operation of the transactional system which the family represents. Hence, family counseling requires a multi-directional approach. We need to pay attention to the communication patterns, the composition of the group, its status in terms of its stage of development, its cohesiveness, its identity, its goals, its values, and the need response patterns. One can conclude that in determining a differential approach between family counseling versus an individual approach with clients, the basis for judgment depends upon whether it is considered that the problems with which the individual presents himself for intervention are encapsulated mainly within the individual and are affecting him subjectively, in contrast to the individual or individuals who present themselves with problems in their interactional relationship with others. Therefore, in order to understand the situation, it is important to have a sample, or samples, of such social interactions in order to get the broadest view possible of the nature of the problems which have been presented for our study and action.

We are using the term *social functioning* defined[1] as follows: "The goal of social work is the enhancement of social functioning wherever the need for such enhancement is either socially or individually perceived. *Social functioning* in this context designates those activities considered essential for performance of the several roles which each individual, by virtue of his membership in social groups, is called upon to carry out .... although performance requires reciprocal activity, or social interaction, between individual and individual, individual and group, and individual and community."

An example of focusing on social functioning would be as follows: in the situation of a latency age, hyperkinetic youngster, who was brought in for help by his parent, it was found that he had a neurological deficit and needed medication to control the hyperkinesis. It was not until this was handled first that the counselor was able to begin working with him to help him in his adjustment within the family situation. The reactive situation subsided both at home and at school with the use of medication. Whereas in another situation where the family came in about a child-parent problem, upon assessment it was discovered that the problem was in reaction to the tensions within the family situation. Namely, what was happening was that the marital problem was projected on to the children in the family who were harrassed and therefore, were not able to perform academically nor socially. In order to help with this problem, it was necessary to work first with the entire family situation, and then to shift the focus where it actually belonged, in the marital situation.

In a unidimensional approach, the entire focus of treatment is placed on the individual child. Whereas in the use of the eclectic approach, we assess the situation from a broader base including the psychological, the social, the cultural and physical aspects, all of which makes up the transactional system. Using such an approach, we are in a better position to determine where the focus of treatment should be. The clinical interventive aspect is kept open-ended in order to take into account any further developments within the situation. As the intervention continues, we focus on the process as well as on the form and content.

The latter situation which we very briefly outlined above requires a multi-dimensional approach because it is so complex. We need to look at it from every frame of reference that we can muster, in order to understand what has happened. Then we are more likely to be able to enter the life stream of the client's situation in the most effective way possible, and for the greatest benefit of the individuals involved. Therefore, we need to examine the situation from the point of view of what has happened. The process as it is going on now, and how we may best enter into it for the benefit of the affected individuals, is equally important. Hence, we are suggesting an integrated synthesis of approaches in which we utilize as many theoretical frameworks as are available in order to understand the complexity of the situations with which we are dealing, and in order to have as broad a perspective as possible to determine our modes of intervention.

In a differential diagnostic and treatment approach to an understanding of the family situation, we look for an opportunity to observe and understand the family as a unit. Usually we are concerned about the nuclear family, though some of the situations coming to our attention may represent an extended kinship relationship, or an extended family including others than consanguineous members of the nuclear family. Where the major focus is on the nuclear intergenerational family situation, though it may not be feasible, or advisable, or indicated, that the total family be treated as a unit, it is usually helpful to seek an opportunity to observe and study the family situation as a whole, preferably as early as possible in the contact. On the basis of such opportunity, the family counselor is usually in an optimal position to assess, on the basis of his understanding, knowledge, skill and the opportunity available to him, what the total family is experiencing. He then needs to assess what the identified member of the family (on whom the focus as the problem bearer has been made) is experiencing, how this experience relates to the family, and how the family situation relates to the client's behavior.

The family is seen as a unit (1) wherever the focus is on the problem as it affects more than one individual in the family, (2) in order to determine the role which each plays in relation to the problem, and (3) in observing the relation of the problem to the functioning of the family.

Most often when the situation comes to the attention of the family counselor, if it is focused on a problem between the parent and child, we have an opportunity to focus on how the intergenerational relationships are being handled in the family. Here we have a rational basis for encouraging the family to come as a unit in order to give us an opportunity to examine with them how they are operating as a family unit, and how it is affecting all members of the family including the identified, or indexed client. As a result of such a mutual examination, it is usually possible to help the family to identify the problem areas which they have already described and how they are related to other areas that become clearer as the result of the family interview. On the basis of such an examination, it is then possible to begin to reach an agreement with the family as to the areas requiring the most immediate attention and to set up priorities and goals in order to determine the best approaches to the problems identified.

To illustrate the situation where the entire family had to be seen, we have the family of parents in their middle forties with three children, a fifteen year old daughter, a nine year old daughter and a six year old son. The parents came to the agency to ask for help in relation to their fifteen year old daughter, who had problems in her social adjustment. They were concerned about the fact that she remained at home too much rather than socializing and developing outside interests. As the counselor assessed the situation, she found that a similar problem existed in the marital couple, for they, too, seemed to be isolated from outside contacts and actually unconsciously as well as consciously encouraged the girl's closeness to them. Family interviews were used to help both the parents and the girl understand the interrelationship and the effect this had on their behavior. It became clear that we were dealing with a maturational problem where the parents' way of relating to the adolescent prevented her from reaching out to her peers and learning to socialize. The parents learned that helping this girl effect some separateness from them would be helpful to the younger siblings when they reached their adolescence. The intrapsychic problems in the family members were not touched upon directly but the interactional patterns were helped to shift so as to enable this adolescent girl to socialize more and to feel more comfortable with herself in this process.

In other situations, in addition to, or in place of treating the family as a unit, we may have to focus on the sub-units in the family situation. For example, where the members of the family had had considerable service previously for their problems on an individual basis, they presented the continuing problems of the children. At this point a family interview revealed many of the difficulties in the parent-child relationships. These were dealt with both in family interviews and individual contacts with the children and with the parents. An effort was made to clarify the nature of the problems that they had and to give them support to deal more directly with the situation in the family interviews. This also involved seeing the parents jointly to discuss with them some of their marital difficulties in communicating with each other. The children were seen to discuss their common problems in multiple interviews as well as their individual problems in individual contacts. Assistance was given to the family to change alliances between the parents and the adolescent children in order to give them better bases for identification among the father and the sons, and the mother and the daughter. This would be an example of the use of an individualized series of approaches to the family as a unit, its sub-systems, and the individuals comprising the family as a means of dealing with the complexities of the situation and of dealing with the problems of the sub-units and the family as a unit in order to help them function more adequately. In the latter situation, the parents were also seen in order to help them understand better how their behavior was affecting the children and how they might handle this more effectively. It was more helpful to see them alone to discuss this area in order to avoid undermining the parents' authority with the children. Consequently, the counselor could be more direct with them.

In contrast, at times, one could start with a conjoint approach to a couple who bring their problem focused on the marriage. For example, a couple came about their difficulty in management of their finances and their budget, and the great differences of attitudes they had towards money which seemed to reflect their general incompatible relationship with each other at this point. When their only child returned home from the university shortly thereafter, she was also brought into the interviewing situation and as a result she was able to serve in a therapeutic capacity to re-establish a balance between her parents. The father would not permit his wife to involve herself in his business. However, he permitted the daughter to do so and this satisfied the mother's need for the family to be closer to what was happening in the business. They were then able to work out a compromise about the handling of money and their interrelationships with each other. The family situation was again balanced on a workable basis. Thus, the approach which started with a focus on the marriage was handled through the medium of total family counseling and a workable balance in the family which previously had been missing was re-established. In this case, it was not necessary to deal with the underlying problems in the marital situation since they came at a time of crisis. The daughter upon re-entry into the family, acted as a co-therapist in helping the parents to look at their situation more realistically and to re-establish the balance of which they were capable with her help and with the counselor's help. As a result, the stress in the situation was relieved and with this came relief of the external pressures which the family was experiencing. They were then able to manage effectively again.

The use of multiple interviews in which the counselor sees more than one individual in the family, as illustrated above, might involve the family as a whole unit, or as parts of the family and its sub-systems. Conjoint treatment of the parents would be another example of a multiple interview with a sub-system as would be those where siblings might be seen because they share common problems. Also intergenerational combinations of one or both parents and one or more children might be seen. This would depend upon the particular situation and the aspects of the problem with which the counselor is helping the clients.

A dyadic relationship between the worker and one person in the family, is present in any situation where the problem is more subjective and is thought to be encapsulated within the individual, or where the individual is unable to share his problems in the presence of any other members of his family. The focus, therefore, must be on his subjective reactions to his situation while taking into account as best we can the outside realities with which he has to deal. Wherever others who need to enter into the treatment relationship are involved, one should be free to include them at the appropriate time and in relation to the client's readiness.

An example of exclusive use of a dyadic relationship would be the young adult who comes to the counselor in order to discuss his pending marriage. He is an individual in his late twenties who has had several courtships, none of which had worked out. He was still residing with his family and was dependent upon his relationship with his parents and siblings. At this point, he was ready to be married but had some second thoughts and many doubts about his choice of a mate. In this, his first marriage, he was marrying a woman who had been married before and had children, and he wondered whether this might interfere in his pending marriage. In addition, the circumstances under which he had met her posed a problem for him, since he knew that she had been spending a great deal of time in public places of entertainment and he wondered about her reputation and moral character. His family also had a great deal of question about his choice of a mate. After discussing his questions in great detail, and reviewing all of the circumstances, he decided that he probably would still marry her because he felt a very deep affection for her. He would still try to convince, or at least, inform his family about the basis upon which he was making this decision. He had decided that he had sufficient confidence in his own opinion that he did not feel that his fiancee needed to be involved in the treatment relationship, firstly, because she was not interested in it, and secondly, because he had come in mainly about *his* questions about *his* decision. One would not involve the family members here because this man was quite capable of reaching his own decision to separate himself from his family. One would not want to discourage this belated movement toward independent action unless there was some indication that he was unable to make this decision responsibly, e.g., because of inadequacies or lack of sufficient integrity. There was no basis for reaching such a conclusion in a situation like this where the man took full responsibility for coming for consultation, and for making his own decisions. Also, his focus was entirely upon himself and upon his own subjective reactions to questions with which he wanted the counselor's help. This was the purpose for his making use of the counselor at this time.

In summary, the basis for deciding the use of one or more approaches on the range of treatment modalities on a family counseling to an individual counseling continuum depends on the focus of the presenting problem and the involvement of the clients in this problem. As we view the individual and/or his family in operation, we evaluate which problems have the highest priority, and determine the interventive modalities on that basis.

Range of Choices in Determining the Use of Family Counseling and Individual Counseling Processes

The continuum of choices starts from one extreme in which an individual presents himself to the counselor with problems which he describes as being subjectively experienced and which he sees mainly within himself. Even though the external environment is seen as impinging upon him and affecting his adjustment, he focuses mainly upon his own involvement in the problem. In such circumstances one would ordinarily select an individual approach in which the counselor would meet with the person requesting the counseling to determine the nature of the problem and the modality of treatment. On the other end of the continuum would be those situations where an individual or several individuals present themselves indicating that they are members of a family which is experiencing difficulty in managing and getting along with one another, in coping with their common problems, or in coping with the problems of one or more members of the family. Some may have problems wherein they are having difficulty with others outside of the family, e.g., in the community, at work, or at school. Here we would ordinarily decide, whenever possible, to see the whole family as a unit in order to determine the nature of the family system, how it is operating, what is the locus and the nature of the difficulty they are experiencing, and what would be the treatment of choice. In between these two extremes we have a whole range of possibilities. First, we may find that the problem initially presented is not the most urgent, or the top priority problem which needs attention. Second, we may find that the problem really lies elsewhere, or with someone else, or with some others. Third, we may discover that only part of the problem has been presented, or that it bears a different interpretation on further examination. In any event, we may choose any approach, from focusing on one individual in the family to the total family as indicated previously, or parts of the family system such as sub-units like the spouses, the parent-child, the siblings, or others in the family situation. We might have different groupings of different members and parts of the family for examination, for assessment, and for intervention or treatment.

In problems which are focused on one of the children in the family, we very often find that though this child may actually have a problem, some other child in the family may have a similar one, or a more complex one which also requires attention, or perhaps should have some priority.

Here, it is important to see the whole family in operation in order to get a more balanced picture of where the stresses lie, to what degree they are in need of help, what is involved in the current balance in the family, and what needs to be done to bring about a more effective balance. An example of this kind of situation is one in which a parent presented a problem as her own subjective problem over a long period of time. It was only when the child, who was of even greater concern to her, and to the community, finally was revealed as the source of a lot of the mother's own distress, that he was seen to be the focus of the problem. In such a situation it might have been helpful had we also requested as part of the initial evaluation of the individual's subjective stress to see the family in operation in order to determine whether the stress was entirely internal, or whether there were factors in the immediate environment and elsewhere playing an important part. There also might be situations where after seeing the family as a whole we may find it essential to see sub-units, for example, where some members of the family use themselves in order to create conflict and destructive attacks among other members of the family, such as the children playing off one parent against the other, or the parents playing off one child against the other. In these situations it is sometimes necessary to see the individuals in order to work on the problems which they are presenting in their relationship with each other.

In family counseling it very often is important in the early phase to have a home visit for diagnostic purposes. An example would be a situation where the mother applied for help with a five year old boy who had just started kindergarten and who was having a problem in attending school. In a home visit, the boy took hold of the counselor's hand in an effort to show her his room and the sleeping arrangements of the remaining members of the family. He very casually remarked that his daddy does not always come home to sleep. In response to the counselor's comment, the boy stated that he overheard his mother tell this to his maternal grandmother. He was, therefore, afraid that his mother, too, might not come home and as a result he did not want to go to school.

It is readily seen how this home visit helped to clarify the situation and enabled the counselor to use this with the family.

Family Counseling as a Total Process of Study, Diagnosis and Treatment

Family counseling offers us the opportunity to view the situation brought to the counselor from a more over-arching point of view as a Gestalt. The individuals may be viewed in terms of the effectiveness of their social functioning. As illustrated previously, family counseling can be used for any aspect of the total process of counseling. It may be part of the study, the assessment phase, or the modality of treatment. As a diagnostic tool, family counseling attempts to assess the individual's functioning on the basis of his carrying out his social roles and his individual functioning within them. This serves as a basis for psycho-social evaluation of the problem presented to the counselor and of the reciprocal relationship between the individual's functioning and that of the other individuals in his immediate environment. Here we focus on the reciprocal relationships the individual has and the degree of congruence not only within himself as a functioning system, but also between himself and others. It is here that one decides, in evaluating the situation, the most effective means of helping the client to deal with the situation. The treatment possibilities are manifold and depend for their emphasis on the situation as well as the particular framework from which the counselor is operating. As indicated earlier, we believe the counselor should operate from an eclectic framework in which he takes into account all sources of information and bases for interpretation of the situations which are presented for his counsel. The factors would include social, biological, cultural, and psychological factors. The list of such factors are legion and appear in many studies, including those cited in the bibliography.

Factors to be Considered in Making a Family Diagnosis

In working with the family, there are three areas which we must consider: (1) a clear definition of the problem;

(2) the nature of the social functioning both of the family and of each individual within the family constellation; (3) the nature of the interaction within the transactional system of the family. In order to assess the interaction, we must understand the strengths of the family, the stage of development both in the family's life cycle and the stage of development of the individual members. The counselor must also review the stress situations which they are experiencing currently, as well as the ways in which they coped with stress situations in the past. In addition to this, we must understand the roles which are assumed or ascribed in the family by the family members, the role expectations they have of one another, how congruent or how compatible they are and the role deficits within the family situation. We must also become familiarized with the family's goals. What are their aspirations as a group as well as for the individual members? How closely do these match, and what problems are precipitated in that area? Very important in work with any family is to arrive at an understanding of the communication patterns and to determine whether these are clearly expressed and understood by the various members of the family. In addition, it is important to find out whether there is freedom of expression and whether individual needs are given consideration. Of equal importance is an understanding of how needs are satisfied and the nature of the family's needs as well as the needs of each individual within the family constellation. How cohesive is the family? What kind of identity do they have? How do they fit into their sub-cultural and into their ethnic groups or religious groups? What coping mechanisms have they used in the past to deal with stressful situa-

tions? What types of problems have they encountered in the past?

It is also important to understand the physical conditions of the various members of the family for that often affects the modality of treatment. The intellectual capacity of the members of the family plays an important role as does their capacity for involving themselves in the treatment process and their motivation for working on the problem as a family group or in combinations as is diagnostically indicated in any particular situation. Viewing the structure of the family is important in terms of determining what the excesses or deficits are since very often the roles assigned to the various individuals within the family are affected by the structure of the family itself. The alliances, splits and collusions are very frequently observed in the initial phases of contact with families and it is important to understand how deep-seated these are. In attempting to define the problem, it is important to assess to what generation the problem belongs, and to see if various generations are involved, for this too will determine the focus of the counseling process.

Content Versus Process Emphases

In family counseling, as in other counseling, it is important to pay attention to the content, or factual data, relating to the situation as well as to the process of counseling. This refers to the fact that in the study and assessment processes, it is important to gather factual information about the development and history of the presenting problems of the individuals involved. Though such material may be gathered in the course of the total counseling process, it is important to gather sufficient information in the beginning so that one may have better understanding of the situation.

Where the clients involved are more able to verbalize about their situation, to introspect and to consider, it is usually desirable to focus on the content of the situation and their considerations about its impact on them. In situations where clients are more prone to acting out, it is usually more productive to focus largely on the interaction among the individuals in the process of the transactional system. In all situations it is important to consider both the content and the process. The emphasis, however, will vary from situation to situation depending upon the development and adjustment of the persons involved. From our point of view, it is advisable to maintain a broader either/or orientation in this respect, since one must usually take into account both content and the process of what is being presented in the family counseling situation. At best, it is a matter of emphasis and degree, and at most, either one or the other may represent the leading theme in the counseling process.

Hence, in the family situation which has as its major feature, disorganization and chaotic family relationships, it is usually important to focus on what is going on among the individuals involved and their external environments, to help them consider the cause and effect aspects of their behavior on each other in the here and now situation with the hope that eventually they will be able to develop some capacity for reflection, and consideration of the situation prior to action.

In contrast, in dealing with a family that tends to follow rigid patterns of behavior and has as its characteristic inflexibility, or narrowness and constriction, it is important to help them consider cause and effect relationships in past, present, and future circumstances. This emphasis is related to a point made by Ivan Boszormenyi-Nagy[2] in which he stresses the transactional nature of the relationship theory emphasizing the importance not only of the psychic economy, but also the nature of the interpersonal relationships which the organism experiences from birth on, as determining the need satisfaction patterns which the individual develops. Consequently the kind of mold and template relationships that he seeks and develops result in meeting his needs for complementarity and mutuality in his interpersonal relationships. This is further support of the emphasis that in order to understand the individual and his needs one has to see him in his environmental situation and deal with the environmental situation in working towards correction of maladaptive responses. Since the significance and intensity of relationship in the family situation is usually of greatest moment in terms of dysfunctional problems which are presented to us for intervention, it is most important to assess and work with them in their natural habitat of the family as a transactional system.

To illustrate this is the case of a young woman, who recently was divorced from her husband, and who came to the agency to seek help in relation to her thirteen year old boy who was showing behavioral difficulties at home and academic problems in school. The interview revealed the fact that the mother was transferring her dependency needs from the husband on to the boy whom she expected to take over responsibilities for disciplining the younger children, helping her with the household chores and baby-sitting whenever she needed to go out. Some of these responsibilities were new and quite taxing for the boy but the mother, out of her own dependency needs, was unable to see this. As she began to discuss the situation, it became quite evident that she was focusing chiefly on factual material. The boy who was also present in the interview looked very uncomfortable, kept his eyes downcast and had little to add. The worker, however, when she noticed his discomfort related to this, discussed this non-verbal bit of communication with him, thereby involving him in the interview. It was at this point that he was able to say rather freely that he felt overburdened by the new responsibilities which his mother expected him to undertake. This was the first time that the mother was able to become aware of this and was helped to see the effect her unrealistic expectations had on the boy.

In this situation it was clearly seen how the process illuminated the content, and the worker by dealing with the *here* and *now* was able to relate to the interaction and help the mother effect some change in the situation. In this example we can see how the worker in relating to the process (the non-verbal communication of the boy) was able to get some content in terms of helping to clarify what the reality of the situation was, namely, that his mother was expecting him to carry certain responsibilities for which he was not quite prepared at his age. This shows the interaction between content and process, and how one relates to the other.

The Need for Administrative Support and a Theoretical Framework for Family Counseling

As in any other form of counseling practice in an

agency or bureaucratic setting, it is important that the setting support the approach to the task and that this support take tangible form such as the following.

First, one assumes that the range of problems being brought to the attention of the counselor usually involves not only the person presenting the problem, or identified as carrying the problem, but also has to involve those in his immediate environment, namely, the family. It is, therefore, important to have physical facilities available that adequately accommodate groups of varying sizes so that the needs of such family groups can be met accordingly for multiple interviews, family unit interviews, and conjoint interviews, as well as for individual interviews. Second, it is important that the schedule of the counselors or the counseling agency be such that it would permit all members of the family group to have access to the counseling hours, such as having different times of the day as well as evening appointment time available. Third, the agency needs to provide opportunity for the counselor to hold counseling sessions outside of the agency setting such as in the home, observational experiences at different sites such as the school, places of employment, or wherever the client requests the counselor to see him in action. Fourth, for those members who occasionally have to be separated out from multiple interviews or family interviews, such as some of the children, provisions need to be made for occupying them in play, or giving them some supervision in a reception area. Fifth, one must have adequate means of recording, such as audio-visual equipment, wherever possible, to record the audio aspects of the interview. Occasionally, it is desirable to record the visual situation for purposes of study and better availability of such material to understand the complexities of the processes involved. Sixth, since many counselors have been trained largely with an individual orientation, in-service training and special arrangements with professional educational centers should be arranged for purposes of training in the family-focused treatment approach. Seventh, adequate provision should be made for research and evaluation of this approach. Eighth, adequate consultation as well as teaching opportunities should be available for training in this approach.

In terms of the theoretical framework, the authors would stress the importance of an eclectic approach utilizing the emphases from all the theoretical frameworks contributing to an understanding of the family, the dynamics of its operations, the behavior of its members and the operation of the family as an open-ended transactional system. This requires that the counselor, although he may have certain predilections for one theoretical framework or the other, needs to remain open-minded to the contributions of all theoretical frameworks in order to acquire knowledge and experience that is rapidly flowing into this field about this approach. Such an attitude will give us the broadest point of view about the family, its mode of operation, and how we may best intervene in behalf of those families and its members whose adaptations in the family situation are maladaptive, and, therefore, contribute to family dysfunctioning.

Since we view the family as a system, we need to look at it both structurally and functionally. Structurally we need to take into account its composition as a unit, something about the origins of the family, about the past experiences of the spouses, their stage of maturation and its relation to their life experience. We must have some understanding of the way in which the spouses became acquainted, how they got together, what their expectations were of each other and of the marriage, and what their relationships are. We then need to explore the meaning of the entry of others into the relationship, namely, children and others who may comprise the family. This would include both the current membership of the family and past membership, and also deficits and excesses in relation to the typical nuclear family composed of the two generational model.

After examining the family structurally in this fashion, we need to examine its present operational and functional relationships, how it operates as a system and in its sub-systems, and how the members relate to the wider environment, both individually and as a group. We also need to pay attention to both the family's sense of identity and that of its individual members. We need to learn something about the value system of the family, the goals they set for themselves, how they carry out their specific social roles, the appropriateness of these roles, and the interrelationships of the role network comprising the family. We then must assess the behavior of the members in relation to their position in their individual life cycles, and also in relation to the life cycle of the family as a viable group. We have to take into account the social realities, the living situation, the economic situation, and the ethnic, religious, and cultural situation, and how the family relates to the larger community in which they are living and functioning. We also need to observe how they relate to extended kinship members of the family, as well as people outside of the extended kinship. In terms of assessing the functional level of the family, we assess not only the functioning in terms of normative standards but also in terms of deviations which contribute to dysfunctional aspects of the family and its members' behavioral functioning. The mode of dysfunctional behavior would be the way in which the family handles not only need satisfactions, but the distribution of power, authority, decision-making, discipline and controls, socialization, encouragement of growth and maturation, or the encouragement of pathological deviant behavior and development. Also in terms of interaction among the family members, we are concerned about their communication patterns, how feedback operates in relation to communication and the response of the individual members to this framework.

In terms of preparing the family for the necessary understanding of a family-focused counseling approach, it is important that we utilize our understanding of the basis upon which the family has been brought to our attention. Who is involved in the initial contact? How may they best be helped to cooperate in developing greater understanding of how the family operates? How may the problem for which they came for counseling be most effectively approached and treated?

Footnotes

¹. As Defined in the Social Work Curriculum Study published by the Council on Social Work Education, 1959, in the Vol. I entitled "Objectives of the Social Work Curriculum of the Future," p. 46.

² Chapter II, A Theory of Relationships, Experiences and Transactions, **Intensive Family Therap,, Theoretical and Practical Aspects,** Ed. Ivan Boszormenyi-Nagy and James L. Framo, Hoeber Medical Division, Harper and Row Publishers, 1966.

References

Ackerman, Nathan W., **The Psychodynamics of Family Life**, Basic Books, Inc., New York 1958, Chap. 9, pp. 138-147.

Ackerman, Nathan W., "A Dynamic Frame for the Clinical Approach to Family Conflict, **Exploring the Base for Family Therapy**, eds., Nathan W. Ackerman, F. L. Beatman and S. N. Sherman, Family Service Association of America, New York, 1961, p. 58.

Ackerman, Nathan, and Marjorie L Behrens, "The Home Visit as an Aid in Family Diagnosis and Therapy," **Social Casework**, January 1956, Vol. 37, No. 1, pp. 11-14.

Ackerman, Nathan W., Frances L. Beatman, and Sanford N. Sherman, **Expanding Theory and Practice in Family Therapy**, Family Service Association of America, New York, 1967, pp. 59-108.

Berne, Eric, **Transactional Analysis in Psychotherapy**, Grove Press, New York, 1961.

Boszormenyi-Nagy, and James L. Framo, **Intensive Family Therapy, Theoretical and Practical Aspects**, Hoeber Medical Division, Harper and Row Publishers, New York, 1966.

Family Service Association of America, **Casework Treatment of the Family Unitl** New York, 1965.

Family Service Association of America, **Casebook on Family Diagnosis and Treatment**, New York, 1964.

Family Service Association of America, **Casebook on Family Treatment Involving Adolescents**, New York, 1967.

Goodwin, Hilda N., and Emily H. Mudd, "Indication for Marriage Counseling. Methods and Goals," **Comprehensive Psychiatry**, October 1966, Vol. 7, No. 5.

Gottlieb, Werner, and Joe H. Stanley, "Mutual Goals and Goal-Setting in Casework, **Social Casework**, October 1967.

Hearn, Gordon, **Theory Building in Social Work**, Toronto: University of Toronto Press, 1958.

Lucas, Leon, and Ruth L. Goldberg, "Teaching Differential Family Diagnosis and Treatment." Unpublished Paper. Presented at the 44th Annual Meeting of the American Orthopsychiatric Association, Washington, D. C., March 23, 1967.

Pollak, Otto, and Donald Brieland, "The Midwest Seminar in Family Diagnosis and Treatment," **Social Casework**, July 1960, Vol. 42, No. 7.

Pollak, Otto, "A Family Diagnosis Model," **Social Service Review**, March 1960, pp. 19-31.

Satir, Virginia, **Conjoint Family Therapy**, Science and Behavior Books, Inc., Palo Alto, California, 1968.

Scherz, Frances, "Multiple-Client Interviewing: Treatment Implications," **Social Casework**, Vol. 43, No. 3, March 1962, p. 120.

Scherz, Frances, "The Crisis of Adolescence in Family Life," **Social Casework**, Vol. 48, No. 4, April 1967, p. 209.

Vogel, Ezra F., and Norman W. Bell, "The Emotionally Disturbed Child as the Family Scapegoat," **A Modern Introduction to the Family**, eds., Ezra F. Vogel and Norman W. Bell, The Free Press of Glencoe, Illinois, Glencoe, Illinois, 1960, pp. 382-398.

Wynne, Lyman, "The Study of Intrafamilial Alignments and Splits in Exploratory Family Therapy," **Exploring the Base for Family Therapy**, eds., Nathan W. Ackerman, F. L. Beatman, and S. N. Sherman, Family Service Association of America, New York, 1961, pp. 95-115.

Young, O. R., "A Survey of General Systems Theory," **General Systems Yearbook of the Society for General Systems Research**, Vol. 9, 1964, pp. 61-80.

SECTION II

TEACHING FAMILY COUNSELING

CHAPTER V

ORIENTING THE SOCIAL CASE WORK STUDENT TO THE FAMILY COUNSELING APPROACH

Evidence from the experience of those who have been teaching family counseling shows that the family-focused approach needs to be introduced early in the professional education of the students with emphasis on the dynamics of family life and behavior, stressing the social realities of family life and of neighborhood and community aspects. The family counselor needs to learn early how he relates himself to these aspects and the agency which he represents, and also to the community responsibilities for supporting and encouraging the development of healthy, functional family units. Hence, in the professional education of the counselor, it is important to teach not only the psycho-social aspects of an individual's behavior but also family models of behavior in relation to the study, assessment and mode of intervention aspects of the counseling process. A psycho-social approach involves a total Gestalt of bio-socio-psychological aspects as well as the cultural aspects of the individual and of the family unit as the unit of attention in the counseling process. In both the class and field experiences of the student of family counseling, it is important that the theoretical and practice frameworks include a family focus and make it possible for the student to experience and have opportunities for utilizing a family-focused approach. This would require opportunities for having an adequate theoretical framework included in his academic preparation and also opportunity for observing and dealing with family situations.

It is important that he be taught perspective about the intrinsic relationship between a transactional and an individual theoretical approach to human behavior and that this focus permeate the entire educational program. Hence, in teaching the relational aspects of human behavior in regard to the mode of intervention and treatment as well as in understanding the behavior of the clients, it should be stressed that the counselor should take into account his relationship to both the individual members of the family and the family as a whole. This he could learn through developing the capacity for observing behavior involving psychological factors, and for being alert to and giving attention to specific aspects of the situation which would provide the data necessary to make the observation. Observation requires accuracy which depends upon the proper use of perception and sensory responses to the situation. This leads to perceiving the appropriate factors that are involved. The observer should take into account his frame of reference, his particular stance, biases and background including values, and his physical, emotional, and intellectual capacity for perceiving behavioral data. Finally, he should be clear about the data he needs in order to achieve the goals for the problem-solving activity in which he is engaged.

The observer must also be aware of the communication aspects of the transactional systems that he is studying in the family and among the individuals involved. He should understand the transactional system in relation to the social role network in the family, to the goals and values of the family, how their needs and satisfactions are met, and to the transference, cross-transference and counter-transference aspects of the responses of the individuals involved, including the counselor.

The counselor also serves as an activator and enables the family to enlarge its capacity to observe itself and to become more aware of the behavior which makes counseling necessary. He helps move the attention from the identified client to the more appropriate sources of the conflicts in the problems presented and to deal with them in appropriate fashion. He also serves as the reflector of the behavior and interactions that are going on among the individuals that are involved. He is a resource person giving knowledge and information, helping them to be aware of the process of their interaction as well as the meaning of the content of what they are doing and communicating. The counselor also serves as a model for the individuals communicating with each other and demonstrates how they may deal with the behaviors which they are presenting to him. He supports them in their efforts to improve the functioning of the family and to encourage the growth and development of the individual members, and of the family as an operating unit. The student must be taught not only to make these observations but also to use proper methods for recording, whether it is in written form or through audio-visual mechanisms, so that the results of his activity can be utilized for purposes of study and better comprehension of the process with which he is working.

References

Hollis, Florence, ".....And What Shall e Teach?" The Social Work Education and Knowledge, **Social Service Review**, Vol. 42, No. 2, June 1968, pp. 184-196.

Satir, Virginia, **Conjoint Family Therapy**, Science and Behavior Books, Inc., Palo Alto, California, 1968.

CHAPTER VI

DIDACTIC TEACHING IN THE CLASSROOM

In Chapter II, the historical background of family counseling is described and is the basis for the introduction to this content. Classroom teaching entails the use of lectures, discussions, oral presentations on reviews of the literature, discussions of case records illustrative of concepts and principles of practice as well as records drawn from the students' practicum experiences; videotapes, audiotapes, direct observations, films, role playing, written assignments are other media used. Seminar discussions of practice and theory summarize the content covered at the end of each of the two graduate years.

We teach historically that social work's more recent interest in family-centered approaches stemmed from the Community Research Associates studies in Hennepin County, Minnesota, San Mateo County, California, and in Washington County, Maryland where they studied respectively the economically indigent, the behavior disordered and medically indigent client groups, one topic respectively in each of these places. Out of this grew the theoretical framework for the so-called hard to reach, hard-core, multi-problem families, the aggressive casework approach, and the realization that it was necessary to deal not only with the specific problems brought to the attention of the agency for service, and not only with the specific clients who made application, but rather with as much of the total situation as was possible. This led naturally into an expanded framework in social casework which included total family situations and the social situation in which the family found itself. Also, this approach followed some of the work done in relation to the Curriculum Study of the Council on Social Work Education which was published in 1959 where the concern of social work was spelled out as being with the social functioning of clients, groups and community situations.

In addition to the Community Research Associates material and the family-centered approach which they emphasized, additional contributions to this approach are reviewed as coming from such centers as the Family Mental Health Clinic of the Jewish Family Service of New York where their particular emphasis under the direction of Ackerman, Gomberg, Beatman, Sherman, Leader, Michell, et al, was developed. This material is described in books such as Ackerman's *Psychodynamics of Family Life*, the FSAA volumes on *Exploring the Base for Family Therapy, Expanding the Theory of Family Treatment*, and Ackerman's later book, *Treating the Troubled Family*.

Other developments are described such as those taking place at the Palo Alto Mental Research Institute in California where they placed particular emphasis on the application of communication theory, and in the developments under the McCormick Fund Project later called the Midwest Committee of FSAA on Family Diagnosis and Treatment under the leadership of Frances Scherz, Otto Pollak, Donald Brieland, etc.; the work of the New Orleans group under Weiss and Munroe; the work of John Elderkin Bell; the work of the Yale group (Lidz, Fleck, et al); and the Harvard group as exemplified by John Spiegel and his contributions with special emphasis on role theory; the transactional theory group as described by Roy Grinker in his book, *Psychiatric Social Work*; Eric Berne's work on transactional analysis; Kurt Lewin's work on field theory; cybernetics and information theory; and the influence of ego-psychology as exemplified by the writings emanating from Smith College such as *Ego-Oriented Casework*, and *Ego-Psychology and Dynamic Casework*; and the inauguration of the *Journal of Family Process* in March of 1962. In addition to these developments, we review the report from the Group for the Advancement of Psychiatry on *Integration and Conflict in Family Behavior* which was first published as Report #27 by the Committee on the Family in August 1954. In our teaching we expand our horizons beyond the psychoanalytic *Weltanshauung*. We demonstrate the greater awareness based on the avalanche of findings that are descending upon us from the social sciences which, in turn, influenced the family counseling field to renew its interest in the social environment of the individual and in the interaction between the individual and his reference groups, with special emphasis on family.

It is known not only from the authors' own experiences but from national experience which is shared at meetings like the annual meetings of the American Orthopsychiatric Association, that the introduction of a family focus is a most difficult innovation. First, there is the strong conviction that people in the helping disciplines have had that the individual approach is the major and most basic approach. Second, there is a great deal of reservation about shifting to a broader gauged focus such as is involved in family diagnosis and treatment. Third, there is criticism that it is difficult enough to learn how to work with an individual much less to expose the students to working with a multiplicity of individuals.

Other methods in social work such as group work and community work have always approached groups rather than individuals, and social casework has always been concerned with the family. More than thirty years ago, one of our basic human behavior texts was Flugel's *Psychoanalytic Study of the Family*. Thus, family counseling has always been family-focused. However, the counseling approach was so influenced by psychoanalytic theory and practice, that family counseling tended to follow very closely the medical model developed by Freud and his followers, and almost completely used an individually-focused approach. It, naturally, will take quite some time before a more varied repertoire of approaches such as is represented by family diagnosis and treatment, which expands the armamentarium of treatment modalities, will become more widely practiced.

Another large area of exploration of the family modality of study and treatment taught comes from the field of experimentation in the area of schizophrenia. There are several centers where this has been particularly studied in depth and extensively; namely, the Yale University setting with Lidz, Fleck, et al, and the National Institute of Mental Health Research Center in Bethesda, Maryland, (1954-1959)[1] where Lyman Wynne, Murray Bowen, et al, have studied schizophrenia in the family milieu following an earlier effort at the Menninger Clinic, 1949-1954.[1]   Out of this experimentation and also from the work at Palo Alto Mental Research Institute came the whole area of the schizophrenogenic characteristics of the milieu. Among the colleagues of Lyman Wynne mentioned above, Murray Bowen especially emphasized the hypothesis that the schizophrenic patient's symptomatology was symptomatic of pathology in the family as a whole. The patient may also have his own pathological reactions, though we may not be able to determine which came first, the chicken or the egg, namely, the schizophrenic reaction or the pathological reactions of the family members. However, he hypothesized that they are interacting in the transactional system of the family. He has stressed especially the concept called the principle of pervasiveness of family disturbance by Pollak (1960),[2] namely, that if one member in the family hurts, everybody else does, which Bowen described as part of "the undifferentiated family ego mass." Bowen believes that the family represents a unitary transactional system in which whatever happens to any portion of the family affects all the others.

Otto Pollak's model (1960)[2] of the typical American nuclear family is used. This model stems from a systems point of view following general systems theory influence in the family diagnosis and treatment framework. In Pollak's emphasis on the three sub-systems of the spouse system, the parent-child system, and the sibling system, the need-response patterns are taught as is the principle of the pervasiveness of family disturbance. This includes the description of the functioning of the family as a system. All parts of the system are affected by whatever influences and stresses affect the family. Pollak's description of the principle of indeterminacy, is also taught. The latter states that the point at which the stress occurs in the family's history will often determine the nature of the response, namely, that if it occurs at a point where the family is more developed in its history it may be better able to cope with it than if it occurs at a time when the family is in a more vulnerable condition. More recently from systems theory, there has been the development of the concept of the equilibrium or homeostatic aspect of the family situation. The latter along

with the family's characteristic coping mechanisms describe how the family maintains its balance. Also taught
is the emphasis of the recent work of the Midwest Committee of FSAA which stresses the importance of the
family roles, goals, strengths and vulnerabilities, need-
response patterns and communication patterns, in diagnosing family situations for purposes of treatment planning. These are emphasized as the aspects of interaction
that need to be considered in diagnosing a family situation.

Also the defense mechanisms such as isolation, along
with tendencies such as prejudice, victimization which
accompanies family conflict, are included in the diagnostic process. Ackerman, in his book *Psychodynamics
of Family Life*, stresses the importance of tracing the
conflict to its source so that the conflict may be brought
back to its origin and the victim of the conflict be relieved. This is another important principle of treatment taught. The concept of identifying the most burdensome problem which has been stressed by Otto Pollak,
Donald Brieland [3] and others in the Midwest Committee
also is important for proper diagnostic determination
of the focus of the problem and the direction where
effort has to be made rather than only being influenced
by presenting symptoms and complaints at the point
of intake.

In studying the interactional aspects of the situation
we are concerned with the functional and dysfunctional
aspects of the family. We emphasize the concepts of
pseudo-mutuality which was a concept coming out of
Lyman Wynne's work at Bethesda. This was further
developed by Ackerman in terms of complementarity,
negative and positive, in family relationships. Here

the stress is important to be understood. Also we need to determine whether or not these aspects of family functioning are represented by realistic perceptions of family relationships in their behavior.

Boszormenyi-Nagy and Framo and others have developed an intensive family treatment theory where they emphasize working through unconscious transferences and distortions in family relationships which they contrast with supportive family therapy focused on enhancing communication and transactional functioning. Bowen has emphasized the importance of the therapist not getting involved in being a healer or repairman,[4] but rather he should be serving as a consultant to the family in the process of their working out their problems. He said one must not allow oneself to become involved in this process. Otherwise, he claimed the clients retreat regressively into dysfunction and maladaptation. On the other hand, there are more directive approaches such as those described by Bardill and Ryan and by John E. Bell who have very specific frameworks for family diagnosis and treatment.

Semantic Considerations in Teaching

The following are some of the terms which we need to define in teaching family counseling. As in much of social work, we must remember that semantics are very important to consider since frequently there is a clearly ambiguous situation which may lead to confusion if one does not define terms adequately. In considering family diagnosis and treatment, we usually think of a family as a unit and are referring to the nuclear family, though most people in this field refer to the nuclear family plus any additions which may be important or significant in the family unit under consideration. Family diagnosis and treatment may involve only an orientation or focus, viewing the diagnosis of the situation from the point of view of the family as a transactional system with an interacting membership. However, the treatment modalities ordinarily used include the family as a total unit and its various parts such as dyads, triads, and pairs of parts of the family. Usually, the FSAA Midwest Committee's definition[5] of family treatment is utilized. It includes some consideration of the family as a totality at some point in order for it to be considered family treatment, namely, at least one interview with the family in some aspect of treatment. However, with some exceptions, one usually considers it possible to use various modalities of treatment from the total group, to parts of the group and individuals. There has to be flexibility of approach in relation to efforts at reaching a differential diagnosis.

Family treatment is variously referred to as family diagnosis and treatment (Midwest FSAA), family unit treatment (Mitchell), family group casework (Bardill and Ryan), family group therapy (John E. Bell), multiple impact therapy (McGregor), conjoint family therapy (Satir), intensive family therapy (Boszormenyi-Nagy and Framo). It is important to define our terms when we are discussing this approach.

Family-centered casework has been defined by Community Research Associates as casework in which social work focuses on helping the family through the utilization of community resources and community interaction in a unified way. *Family-focused casework* focuses on the family *per se* as defined by Scherz and others. A *family* consists of blood related, or legally related members, functioning and living as a family unit. *Family diagnosis and treatment* as we use it refers to the fact that the counselor starts with the family as the focal point of study and intervention, and works through various modalities appropriate to the situation and in relation to the need and readiness of the individuals involved. This is based on the central concept that an individual is not only the recipient of, but also the participant in conflictual areas.

At this point, it is essential to re-emphasize the fact that the importance of the individual-centered approach is not minimized but rather enriched by the family-focused approach. It should be consistently emphasized in the classroom that this is in addition to the client-centered, individual-centered approach and takes into account the transactional system of the client's milieu.

Some of the basic assumptions about human growth and development that should be emphasized in the use of family diagnosis and treatment follow. First, behavior is seen as strongly influenced not only by the intrapsychic processes, like the unconscious, but also by the interaction of one individual with other human beings. This means that a basic psychodynamic, psychosocial orientation is essential in order to be able to relate to understanding the entire family. Second, the family is viewed as a social organization and an open-ended social system, and not as an individual organism such as the client in the individual approach. Third, therapeutic neutrality is maintained in working with a family in contrast to working with individuals when there is more likelihood of the development of transference and counter-transference aspects in individual-centered counseling.

Fourth, in the family treatment situation there is counselor focus on the interaction among the individuals comprising the family. The counselor brings in the possibility of what Celia Mitchell[6] has called cross-transferences, that is, transferences to the client's situation and those of the client's extended family. Fifth, is the family's basic cross-generational situation and its influence on the nuclear family. Sixth, the family is composed of an interacting and interdependent membership and has the characteristics of a small group in terms of its cohesiveness, morale, goals and values, decision-making, authority relations, membership, coping mechanisms, and power structure.

Teaching in Class

With the preceding framework as a philosophical and theoretical base for this approach we continue in our classroom teaching to discuss the application of this framework in practice. This follows the usual study, diagnosis, treatment model in which we discuss ways and means of gathering data in a family situation; the fact that we need to observe the interaction among the family members, their behavior, verbal and non-verbal; the fact that the family treatment approach requires, at least, one total family unit interview, usually, where we observe the family in process and also, if possible, a home visit to see the family in its natural environment. In observing the interaction, we look for direct means of communication as well as pathological forms of communication such as the well-known double bind, confusions, vagueness, ambiguity, contradictions, congruence and incongruence of messages, adequate and inadequate delivery of messages, feedback of messages and meaning, and forms of adequate and inadequate communication.

In our teaching, we help the student begin to view the family in operation within its interactional processes in the transactional system. Emphasis is placed on the functioning of the family. The focus, therefore, must be on the process as well as content in the interactions within the family and with the worker. The role of the worker is to serve as receiver and reflector to the family of the process that is taking place in the family. The worker also serves as a resource person and a model for communication and interaction. With the more primitive or naive family the process is more significant than the content; with the more sophisticated family much of the focus must also be on the content.

For the purpose of diagnosis, we teach the student that study, diagnosis and treatment are simultaneous processes. He is taught to examine and assess the family structure and composition, its formation, its environment, the operation of the social role network, the biological, psychological and social levels of functioning, the stage in which the family is in its life cycle and its history, its equilibrium and coping resources, as well as evidences of dysfunctioning. The level of functioning of the family depends on the functioning of its own sub-systems as well as the functioning of the total system. We also seek evidences of family dysfunctioning according to the Pollak model described above.

In treatment, the intervention depends on where the dysfunctioning lies, whether it is in the area of structure which requires repair or adaptation, or whether it is related to disturbances, regression or arrest in growth or maturational processes, or in the functional processes in terms of its role network, its attitudes, its values, its goals, or its system of informing and transmitting messages and meanings. The family may be helped in repair of its functioning, in enabling them to secure and utilize outside resources as well as their own resources.

On the basis of our experience thus far, we teach that this approach is applicable to every setting except that the focus may be somewhat different depending on the circumstances of the client and agency situation. Indications and contraindications are taught as described in Chapter I.

Students' Reactions in Classroom Learning

One of the major obstacles to student's family-focused orientation is the persistence of the individual orientation and the medical model of focusing on internal pathology in clients. Broadening of the student's perspective is achieved by the conceptual framework outlined above and by the exposure in class and field to practice-based case illustrations of the place and validity of a family-focused orientation among the treatment modalities learned by the student.

Some of the typical reactions are questions about confidentiality, secrets, neutrality in relationships, the place of family unit versus individual and multiple interviews. The elemental stage of development of some of the theory and the variety of formulations cause confusion for students. Discrepancies in focus among field sites provokes many questions. The continuing novelty of this approach for some causes doubts.

Problems of shifting the focus from scapegoated, or

victimized family members cause concern. The multiplicity and complexity of relationships involved and the often high emotional tension of family interviews cause anxiety and uncertainty for students. Relevance of the approach for all settings and the points of intervention characteristic for each setting create student anxiety.

One area of concern is how to involve the resistive member of the family in the family interview. Second, are the questions aroused by the requirement for involving the asymptomatic family members. Third, is how to maintain continuity. Fourth, is the question of what segment is to be seen, when, how and under what circumstances. Fifth, is a search for scientific validation of this modality of treatment. Sixth, uncertainty about how to apply criteria and contraindications for a family-focused approach is frequent.

Protection of family members encouraged to discuss their conflicted, hostile, aggressive, sexual and other drives cause hesitation about the safety of such an approach. Safeguards for maintaining valid parental authority and integrity of the social roles of all family members are sought by students.

Students may also feel inadequate to deal with family constellations which may reflect unresolved issues in their life situations. Also lack of life experience may hinder their feeling of competence in dealing with client family circumstances.

Dealing With Student Reactions in the Classroom

Consensual validation of other students' experiences, evidence from case records, research and experience reported in the literature and by the instructors, and the student's own clinical experience serve to answer many of the questions mentioned above.

Repetition of theory, concepts and principles and their interrelationships with other learned and experienced models is important in helping the students integrate the family-focused conceptual framework.

Footnotes

[1] Boszormenyi-Nagy, Ivan and James L. Framo. **Intensive Family Therapy,** Chapter 5, Murray Bowen, Family Psychotherapy in the Hospital and In Private Practice. N. Y. Hoeber Medical Division, Harper and Row, pp. 214-215.

[2] op. cit. p.21

[3] Pollak, Otto and Donald Brieland. The Midwest Seminar in Family Diagnosis and Treatment. **Social Casework,** Vol. 42, No. 7, July 1961, p. 319.

[4] Bowen, Murray The Use of Family Theory in Clinical Practice, **Comprehensive Psychiatry,** Vol. 7, No. 5, October 1966, p. 345.

[5] **Casebook on Family Diagnosis and Treatment,** FSAA, New York, June 1964.

[6] Celia B. Mitchell. Integrative Therapy of the Family Unit, **Social Casework,** Vol. 46, No. 2, February 1965, p. 63.

References

Ackerman, Nathan W., **The Psychodynamics of Family Life**, Basic Books, Inc., New York, 1958.

Ackerman, N. W., Frances L. Beatman, and Sanford N. Sherman, **Exploring the Base for Family Therapy**, Family Service Association of America, New York, 1961.

Ackerman, N. W., Frances L. Beatman, and Sanford N. Sherman, **Expanding Theory and Practice in Family Therapy**, Family Service Association of America, New York, 1967.

Ackerman, N. W., **Treating the Troubled Family**, Basic Books, Inc., New York, 1966.

Bardill, Donald, and Francis J. Ryan, **Family Group Casework**, Catholic University of America Press, Washington, D. C., 1964.

Beatman, Frances L., "Training and Preparation of Workers for Family Group Treatment," **Social Casework**, Vol. 45, No. 4, April 1964, p. 202.

Bell, John E., **Family Group Therapy**, Public Health Monograph No. 64 (Department of Health, Education and Welfare), Washington, D. C., 1961.

Berne, Eric, **Transactional Analysis in Psychotherapy**, Grove Press, New York, 1961.

Boehm, Werner, **Social Work Curriculum Study**, Council on Social Work Education, New York, 1959.

Boszormenyi-Nagy, Ivan, M.D., and James L. Framo, Ph.D., eds., **Intensive Family Therapy**, New York, Harper and Row, Hoeber Medical Division, 1965, Chaps. 1, 5, 8.

Bowen, Murray, "The Use of Family Theory in Clinical Practice," **Comprehensive Psychiatry**, Vol. 7, No. 5, October 1966, p. 345.

Family Service Association of America, **Casebook on Family Diagnosis and Treatment**, New York, 1964.

DIDACTIC TEACHING IN THE CLASSROOM

Family Service Association of America, **Casebook on Family Treatment Involving Adolescents**, New York, 1967.

Family Service Association of America, **Casework Treatment of the Family Unit**, New York, 1965.

Flugel, J. C., **The Psychoanalytic Study of the Family**, London, Hogarth Press, 1960, (10th imprinting).

Grinker, Roy S., **Psychiatric Social Work: A Transactional Case Book**, Basic Books, Inc., New York, 1961.

Jackson, Don D., ed., **Communication, Family and Messages, Human Communication**, Vol. I, Science and Behavior Books, Inc., Palo Alto, California, 1968.

Jackson, Don D., ed., **Therapy, Communication and Change, Human Communication**, Vol. II, Science and Behavior Books, Inc., Palo Alto, California, 1968.

Journal of Family Process, The Family Institute, 149 E. 78th Street, New York, N. Y., 10021.

Lewin, Kurt, **Field Theory in Social Science, Selected Theoretical Papers**, Harper and Brothers, New York, 1951.

Lidz, Theodore, Stephen Fleck, and Alice Cornelison, **Schizophrenia and the Family**, International University Press, New York, 1966.

MacGregor, Robert, et al., **Multiple Impact Therapy With Families**, Blackiston Division, McGraw-Hill Book Co., New York, 1964.

Mitchell, Celia B., "Integrative Therapy of the Family Unit," **Social Casework**, Vol. 46, No. 2, February 1965, p. 63.

Parad, Howard J., and Roger R. Miller, **Ego-Oriented Casework**, Family Service Association of America, New York, 1963.

Parad, Howard J., **Ego Psychology and Dynamic Casework**, Family Service Association of America, New York, 1958.

Pollak, Otto, "A Family Diagnosis Model," **Social Service Review**, Vol. 34, No. 1, March 1960, pp. 19-31.

Pollak, Otto, and Donald Brieland, "The Midwest Seminar in Family Diagnosis and Treatment," **Social Casework**, Vol. 42, No. 7, July 1961, p. 319.

Satir, Virginia, **Conjoint Family Therapy**, A Guide to Theory and Technique, Science and Behavior Books, Palo Alto, California, 1968.

Spiegel, John P., "The Resolution of Role Conflict Within the Family," in **A Modern Introduction to the Family**, Ed. by Norman W. Bell and Ezra F. Vogel, The Free Press of Glencoe, Illinois, Glencoe, Illinois, 1960, Chap. 30.

The Group for Advancement of Psychiatry, **Integration and Conflict in Family Behavior**, Report ½27, New York, August 1954.

Voiland, Alice L. and Associates, **Family Casework Diagnosis**, Columbia University Press, 1962.

CHAPTER VII

PRACTICUM

Teaching Family Diagnosis and Treatment in the Field Setting

The family counseling approach as taught in a field work training unit [1] is described on page 131. Caseloads assigned to students in the training unit were of a diversified nature including such problems as marital difficulties, parent-child problems, physical handicaps, alcoholism, severe financial problems and others. An effort was made in the choice of cases to provide each student with at least one or two cases where working with the family as a unit and the use of multiple interviews appeared to be the likely treatment of choice, although this was not always predictable. The emphasis in the unit was on a holistic approach though multiple, joint and individual interviews were used as diagnostically indicated. Among these cases were multi-problem families where there was much indifference towards help, recurrence of need, disorganization and chaotic family life.

Orientation for the students took place in group sessions. As is the usual practice, orientation to agency function, policies and procedures continued in individual conferences in relation to specific cases as well as through student contacts with staff members. Students learned the geographical and physical characteristics of the area served by touring the community by automobile and visiting other agencies.

Individual and group conferences were the chief educational media used in field instruction. The individual tutorial sessions were the major teaching media used in field instruction for developing an educational diagnosis of each student's learning needs and for utilizing the student's practice experiences for his learning. In addition, group conferences were used to review the application of concepts and principles taught in class and applied in the field. The students stimulated each other's creativity and intellectual curiosity, and shared and supported each other's learning. From the very beginning the student was helped to understand that family unit treatment is not the only mode of treatment to which he will be exposed but that he would learn to use it differentially and that this approach enriches the one-to-one approach and is not used instead of it.

Conceptualization about his practice was supported by both forms of instruction and assisted the student's assimilation and synthesis of this knowledge in his daily practice. Students were given the opportunity to listen to taped interviews, to observe interviews, single, joint, family and group, and to participate in regular agency-wide staff meetings. Each student needed help in learning his professional role in interaction with the family as the client, and in integrating this approach with his experiential learning in the field. Here the emphasis was on the practice experience first, with conceptualization flowing from the practice. Basically, there needs to be consistent emphasis on the family unit as the client and not merely on the individual.

The conceptual framework is eclectic. The field instructor teaches a student how to put his knowledge to use. The therapeutic goal is to help individuals and families who are experiencing various problematic situations, which means that the central focus in field work is three-fold—namely, the individual or family, the problem, and ways of helping. The responsibility of the field instructor is to teach how to understand and assess the individual and/or a family and to help the student integrate knowledge and practice. The primary focus is on the interactional processes and transactional system within the family with concentration on the effects of the maladaptive behavior, followed by subsequent consideration of causal relationships, (viz., what, how and then why).

Initially, the student's interviewing skills were limited; the student was frightened. of this approach as he might have been in learning other approaches. The level of anxiety was high and the less experienced the student was the more task-oriented he tended to be. The student was helped to move away from his initial concentration on doing, to examining the family stress presented in the intake process. He was taught how to explore initially what the current situation is.

The student was taught how to observe and listen with a purpose—to understand in order to help. Observation had to be as complete as possible. Sometimes a second student might have sat in as an observer to match his observations with that of the counselor. Important in observation were such factors as appearance, facial gestures, body movements, seating arrangements, emotions expressed, behavior, manner, moods, affect, tone of voice, and in general verbal and non-verbal messages. Students were encouraged to observe the patterns of communication.

The student was taught how to observe and what to explore regarding family interrelationships and interactions in their interviews. The presenting versus the most burdensome problem was examined with the student in relation to case material. Emphasis was placed on the student's observation of interaction, both verbal and non-verbal communication, and how the roles of the various members of the family were carried. How was the presenting problem experienced by various members of the family? What appeared to be the cause of the problem? For what kind of help was the family asking? How did they intend to use it? What were reasonable goals and how could they be achieved? How was this related to agency function? What was the student's role in relation to the family?

As additional material unfolded, the student was encouraged to explore whether the problems experienced by the family were of an interactional nature, or whether these were intrapsychic disturbances disrupting the family functioning. Differential approaches in handling such situations were taught. The student was taught to identify and to respect the client's values, his cultural background and the psycho-social and biological factors involved. Along with this the student was encouraged towards self-awareness and self-control, and helped to recognize counter-transference aspects that might have interfered with his performance. No attempt was made to go into the reasons why the student experienced these reactions except as it related to the particular case situation. The focus was clearly on teaching the student how to function professionally. Every effort was made to create an atmosphere conducive to self-awareness, self-evaluation, trust and free discussion with the field instructor. There was much emphasis on the student's creative use of self with support from the field instructor. He was also taught that there is no one right or wrong way but what was right or wrong for the particular family in question was based on differential diagnostic needs. Much effort was put forth to help the student's interventions gradually become consciously directed activity rather than mainly intuitive.

The student was taught that an essential part of the social study was the home visit where the family can be observed in its own setting. If a full family interview was not possible at home, then such was required in the office before the social study could be completed. Every effort was made to reach out to families by providing evening hours for mutually convenient appointments, encouraging their complete involvement by helping them understand the need as related to the problem.

To be specific—in order to evaluate a family the student was encouraged to assess and understand the family structure both external and internal, and the individuals within the family. Is this a complete family? Is it a one-parent family? What are the roles and goals? What is the physical environment? How do they function intellectually and emotionally? How are the needs of individual members met? What is the developmental history of the family? In other words, in what stage of the life cycle is this family? What are the stresses the family experienced both normal and pathological—as it moved from one stage to the next. What is the socio-economic status of this family? What are their values? Are there value conflicts within the family—between individuals or between family and community? What are the themes or issues in this family? What are the communication patterns like in terms of clarity and congruence? What is the nature of the family equilibrium? What are the coping mechanisms? And what are the pathological mechanisms?

In terms of treatment of a family, just like in the

individual approach, the student was helped to understand that treatment flows from the diagnosis. In other words, it depended from where the problem facing the family originated. Generally, the student was helped to understand that he must relate to the problem areas within the context of the family situation.

The psycho-social study stimulated the student's thinking about how to begin to relate and to use one's self in the relationship with the family. The beginning students started with learning basic methods of communication with clients. Their progress was partly determined by their own life experience. The process described what constituted a professional relationship, what each one put into it, what the expectations were of each individual. The initial emphasis with the beginning student were the basic social work principles and concepts emerging from discussion of case material and their validity for the treatment process. Such principles as, beginning where the client is, taking into account what he is prepared to do for himself, and confidentiality were taught. It was also important to emphasize the need for greater flexibility in terms of the time element for family interviews since these frequently needed to last longer than the customary time for an interview.

Some of the areas for learning which usually were brought in early by the students included how to prepare a family for a family interview, how one relates to a family without taking sides, how to involve all members of a family in the interview, including non-communicative, and/or resistive, hostile clients, how to help the scapegoated, victimized or problem-bearing family members express themselves freely without fear of retaliation from others, and when to use family unit, multiple, joint, or individual interviews. The student's concerns about undermining parental authority and dealing with certain aspects of family secrets came through and were handled directly with him. As the student began to use himself more freely and differentially in interviews, he recognized how multiple interviews were used diagnostically, how these served to sharpen observations and enabled him to translate the meaning of the interactions within the family.

It is of interest to note that as soon as the student began to understand the meaning of the interactional and transactional process in the family, he started to develop increased comfort in the new way of using himself in a family situation, e.g., in helping the family understand and deal with the circular reactions. With this, both the family and the student were able to begin to define together what the problem was. The student proceeded to set up a contract with the family in terms of goals, involvement as to who, when, and where the clients would be seen. He discussed with the family the importance of free communication amongst members without fear of retaliation, especially on the part of children, and emphasized the fact that the family members would be working on the problem and finding their own answers with the student acting as resource person or consultant.

As in all aspects of the practicum, it was important in this learning process for the student to have easy and continuous availability of the field instructor with consistent support to encourage the stimulation and often anxiety-producing challenge that came with family unit treatment. He tested concepts learned in the classroom and applied in practice, as well as made observations about his findings from practice which in turn reinforced theory. The field instructor's own conviction about knowledge and comfort with this approach was **basic** to the teaching situation.

Use of Case in Teaching Application of Concepts and Principles

The following case was used to teach several areas, such basics as (1) preparation for a family interview—especially with resistive members as illustrated here; (2) the difficulty in shifting from single to family interviews; (3) how and what to observe; (4) how to begin to communicate with a family; (5) how to involve the entire family; (6) how to use self in the relationship with the family without taking sides yet supporting the indexed or identified client sufficiently so as to shift the problem to where it belonged within the family.

The M. case was assigned to a second year graduate student upon referral from a teacher of one of the special rooms in a junior high school. The teachers felt that Gregory, age 14, lacked emotional maturity to function in the normal classroom setting. Their assessment of Gregory's maturity level was based upon some of the following kinds of occurrences: Gregory was disturbing in the halls; he made derogatory remarks about "Uncle Toms"; played with infantile toys; showed lack of self-control with tendency towards impulsive behavior, often yelling and screaming at teachers. He tended to "act out" particularly in unfamiliar situations.

This parentless family consisted of four boys ages 10, 14, 16, and 18, under the guardianship of a paternal aunt who was unmarried and middle-aged. The siblings were all in age appropriate grades at school. The paternal aunt lived with the boys in their home in the inner city. The neighborhood was relatively well-kept although the family's home was one of those in disrepair. There was much activity among the boys with other children and adults in the neighborhood with frequent visting between homes. Despite these contacts the aunt said that the neighbors provided very few offers of help after the parents' deaths.

Gregory and his brothers lost their parents recently due to an accidental death. There had been a long history of marital difficulty around the wife's infidelity and her attempts to obtain her husband's commitment. Mr. M. worked steadily in a factory but the family seemed to be in bad financial straits until the last few years. They seemed to have a dependent relationship with the aunt from whom they secured help periodically. At the time of their deaths all the siblings except Gregory were present and there was some indication that Gregory felt guilty about his absence.

The student worked with Gregory individually for almost a month after observing him in the classroom and found that he was presenting bizarre, infantile, impulsive behavior, most of which appeared to be directly related to inadequate resolution of mourning. The case was assigned for family treatment. The diagnostic assessment indicated that the 14 year old boy, by his acting out, was reflecting the unresolved mourning work of the brothers individually and of the aunt. The family scapegoated Gregory with the result that he showed the main presenting problem.

The student had contacted the aunt in preparation for the family interviews. The family's complaints centered on Gregory because of his behavior at home and school. They said he had begun to be uncontrollable before the parents' deaths by refusing to take direction from them and frequently lied. The presenting problem at the time of the student's intervention was recorded by her as being:

> the disruptive effect Gregory was having on the family's attempts towards cohesiveness. His aunt saw his rebellious hostile behavior as a direct attack on her and her efforts to manage for the family during their grief. The two older brothers were able to provide some empathy stating Gregory's problems were ones they had struggled with at his age. They recognized grief was perhaps making adolescence more difficult for him but were able to convey understanding and assurance. The younger brother took a more competitive stance towards Gregory, saying he had more control than the brother who mostly acted like a three year old.

In several interviews that preceded on an individual level the student noted Gregory's strong negative feelings towards the family interview. The student records the following:

> I attempted to relieve some of his anxiety and depression using reflective discussion and sustaining techniques. Basic to Gregory's resistance and anxiety was fear of having to face possible criticism from his family. He sees his position as alienated from his brothers and in a sense feels they had always been disloyal to parents as they are continuing to be now in compliance with the aunt. He seems to have identified closely

with his father as he has often mentioned father's teaching him his skills, his being able to talk with his father and sympathize with him when the rest of the family thought he was crazy.

Gregory's two main defenses against involvement with family sessions were that his aunt organized these, they were *her* interviews and not his or the family's. I tried to handle this by discussion of stresses of mourning, how families can pull apart and his feeling regarding getting family together. Gregory projected his anger toward his aunt saying things would be all right without her, that his brothers would be different. He seemed to be losing control of anger, cursing the aunt, saying that she wasn't going to be able ever to tell him what to do. I left the choice of coming to the interview up to Gregory, saying I was not forcing him to come despite the aunt's demands. I said I wanted him to participate but the decision was his as he would have to feel himself that interviews were helpful.

The other defense Gregory used against family sessions was saying he didn't care about what happened to the family, that he was just biding time to when he could leave. As I pointed out instances of caring he became uncomfortable and seemed on the verge of tears. I supported his feelings by telling him it was a difficult position to be in when he felt everyone picked on him or called him a liar. I explained that if he felt something then factual correctness was not important and his feelings were not lies. I carefully said that I was a stranger, that he needn't trust me but I was being honest in trying to help him and one way was with the family. We talked a little of future plans but at this point I wanted to help him focus on the present reality and motivate him to want to cope with it.

Prior to the family interview, in conference with the student there was discussion of the dynamics of Gregory's behavior, the kind of stress he was experiencing and the meaning it had for him and the family. Obviously this was important to understand no matter what approach was used in the situation. The student was helped to understand the nature of Gregory's resistance, the anger he felt towards the world in general for the sudden and tragic deaths of his parents, his guilt around the deaths, his need to project anger onto the aunt whose rigid management of the household he resented aside from her consistent critical attitudes towards his deceased mother and father, and his difficulty in shifting his object relationships in his search for identity. Even though it was important enough for him to be accepted within the family, his anger and his strong identification with his father were deterrent factors in what appeared to him to be a shift in loyalties. Also operating here was his fear of self-exposure in front of the family which was frequently a basic factor in resistance to family treatment. Here the student needed reassurance around the meaning and importance of her support of Gregory in order to help him understand that the entire family situation had a part in the problems he was experiencing.

It was following several family interviews that the student was able to assess the situation more clearly in terms of the crisis precipitated by the parents' deaths which occurred at an acute period in the family's history with all the boys at various stages of transition into and out of adolescence or latency. Family operations were seen as relatively inflexible and resistant to intervention.

The student recorded the first family interview as follows:

Interview With M. Family

This first family interview was a late afternoon home call. Miss M. greeted me and as we went into the living room there was a lot of shuffling of the boys into the adjoining dining room. I introduced myself to Art and Michael whom I had not met before as they all brought chairs into the living room for the interview. Gregory had to be called out from the kitchen and the family explained with some disgust that he had to be restrained from leaving before my arrival. I sensed they thought that as Gregory was my client he should be present and further that I would want to be talking *about him in the interview.*

I noted that the seating arrangement reinforced this attitude as Gregory was sitting alone at one end of the room and across from him were his aunt, then Glen, Art and Michael, and I was in between alone on the sofa. Also present throughout was Gregory's friend, who sat behind Gregory's brothers almost out of view. In the abstract, the group of us formed a triangle.

Before summarizing the verbal interaction, I will describe the tone of non-verbal communication. Gregory was characteristically hyperactive being unable to sit still in his chair. At those times when family was particularly critical of him, Gregory faced away from all of us or he would stand up and look out of the front window. Miss M. would ask him to sit politely and "talk to the lady" but her comments were always met with no response. Toward the end of the interview when the family began to feel cohesive Gregory participated by getting up, walking all about the room, and moving closer to the others as he talked. It was interesting that Gregory was the most expressive, verbally and non-verbally, of the family with his movements corresponding to the content of the interview as it affected him. As I observed in other situations, Gregory also seemed to derive pleasure from the attention given him and successfully provoked further reactions almost as if to hold the focus on himself. The other family members remained seated and reflected none of the agitation Gregory displayed. I speculated that they may have taken some satisfaction in seeing Gregory uncomfortable and with the boys it may have been displaced release for their own feelings of anger and anxiety toward current situation.

Interview began with my asking each of the family what they thought my job was and what preparation they had had for my coming. They were aware that I was a social worker working with Gregory at the school and my purpose in coming was to help the family in some way.

I gave recognition to the difficult time they had been having since their parents' deaths and said that their aunt had been making every effort to help them stay together but had indicated wanting assistance because there were still difficulties she could not clear up on her own. I further explained that one of the things I did was to help families pull together after such a painful loss of their parents. I pursued a discussion of feelings about being a family with each of them toward the end of setting mutual goals for finding ways to make the family more cohesive.

All except Gregory were responsive to my intervention. When Gregory expressed open indifference and said they were not a family, his brothers, especially Michael and Glen, verbalized feeling that Gregory was one member who was making it difficult for all of them to pull together. They enumerated his childish behavior, his unwillingness to take direction from either aunt or them. Art also participated in attacking Gregory's behavior saying that he often knew better than Gregory even though he was only 10. I let this ventilation go on for a while occasionally asking the aunt to respond as she had been quite silent. Gregory was able to respond in defense of his actions and underlying his statements was a feeling that, since no one really cared for him or even listened to him, he had little motivation to participate with them as a family.

Gregory was becoming increasingly agitated, and as I observed his desire to leave, his friend interestingly began to involve himself in the interview. As Gregory became less responsive and was pacing about his chair, his friend told him that he should sit down and that he was just trying to escape the situation. I felt at this point that Gregory needed an advocate to interpret to the family his covert message of feeling alienated but I also did not want to create a divisive alliance with him. I attempted to relieve pressure by bringing the family's attention to our goal of pulling the family together and saying it might help to look at ways Gregory and family could feel closer.

This opened up a positive direction for family to take and they readily responded at a feeling level. Michael said he could understand why Gregory was acting as he was since he had gone through the same thing at 14. He explained that this was why he always tried to talk to Gregory and steer him away from actions he knew would create problems for Gregory. Glen reiterated Michael's view that at Gregory's age it was natural to be rebellious, to want to be independent, and further to recognize that perhaps Gregory was having a harder time than he or Michael. I shifted focus back to Gregory asking what effect his brothers' statements were having on him. He fidgeted and couldn't say, so I clarified for him saying I heard his brothers saying they cared about him. Gregory responded like a child, squirming and saying he didn't like all that "mush" stuff.

Miss M. then, too, became supportive pointing out jokingly that Gregory didn't seem to mind such mushiness when it had to do with girls. I again clarified for Gregory that we were talking about real feelings and that there was nothing wrong with brothers saying they liked him and this was how families got closer by talking honestly together. The affective tone of family then changed and they continued in support of Gregory each one of them commenting on how relatives, friends, and neighbors enjoyed Gregory's company and how especially capable he was mechanically when he set his mind to doing something. His friend followed family's tone saying his father was really fond of Gregory.

As the family was now showing some cohesion, I said I wanted to know how they went about doing things together and asked about household and household tasks. Glen and Miss M. complained about lack of organization and indifference of other members about how home looked and how they were left with all the work. I elaborated saying families had to have routines, delegation of chores, but that also each had to feel his contribution was worthwhile. Together we discussed their reasons for resistance, how if one cleaned up there was no apparent cooperation from the other. I again attempted to help them see how this related to feeling as a family. We then moved to devising a plan for tasks with each member voicing what rooms they would clean and working out conflicts about preferences. I wrote each of the decisions down and gave

Miss M. the task of supervising as there was question about who would set the standards. They all seemed to be enjoying this process, especially Gregory and Arthur, with Gregory saying each had to keep his word now that it was on paper and with Arthur taking the paper saying they should hang it up for everyone to see.

Gregory then began discussion of how he wanted to paint the house and the idea was tossed around pro and con, how each wanted the house to look. It was decided Gregory could paint in the Spring. The aunt was supportive of Gregory's idea. I ended the interview by reviewing what we had just done saying they had shown real ability to work as family and that I would like to hear from each what he thought of continuing such sessions. Michael, Arthur, and Miss M. quickly responded to my returning and Gregory put up some protest about interviews taking time he could be earning money, although his resistance was not very great. Glen said it didn't matter one way or another and Michael was quick to pick up that such an answer really meant he didn't care. There seemed to be some indication that this was a pervasive attitude for Glen which bothered Michael who wanted his brother to commit himself. Glen insisted he was concerned and wanted family together but again said it didn't matter if I returned if family wanted it. I set another appointment.

The student's impressions following the interview were as follows:

> From this interview it became apparent that Gregory is bearing the brunt of family's suffering and their feelings of loss and separateness since parents' deaths. He is acting upon his feelings of anger for himself and his brothers. It is almost as if they are permitting his behavior, of necessity, to satisfy their own grief, and Gregory's alienation from them speaks of their own separateness from each other.
>
> Their interaction made apparent also that Michael is the group's sensitizer and he is the most willing to speak freely and reflect what he sees is happening. He wants very much to feel the family together and often acted in alliance with me when there was misinterpretation or evasion of problems. Glen holds a rather detached, indifferent attitude toward involving himself and I would speculate he feels burdened and uncomfortable with role of eldest and the expectations of brothers that he lead them. Also it seems he has internalized his grief and his indifference indicates a need to protect himself from these feelings. Arthur who is the youngest identified strongly with the two oldest and goes along with their attitudes toward Gregory. There is also strong sibling rivalry between Arthur and Gregory and I suspect Gregory has been especially punitive and competitive with Arthur. Miss M. was unusually quiet during the interview which I felt was some hostility towards my intervention and her whole involvement with having to care for the family.

My goals for the next few sessions are continued exploration of family's view of problems with focus on sharing these as a family, observing family operations, and showing awareness with them and pointing out effects each has had on the other and, eventually, to shift current negative balance from Gregory.

The student's ability to empathize with Gregory helped him to be more realistic about the situation. She recognized the stresses he was experiencing and the importance of having the support of the family at a critical time like this. She expressed her interest in helping him and his family to be more cooperative, understanding and involved since they, too, were experiencing mourning and separation difficulties. The student made it clear that she wished him to participate in the family interview but had to leave the final decision up to him. She, thus, freed him sufficiently to wish to test out his trust in her. The student recognized the *pervasiveness* of the problem and the concept of what hurts one in the family hurts all—now became very real to her. She, therefore, was able quite effectively, to convey this to Gregory. Yet his ambivalence continued to be apparent in the interviews that followed, but he sensed the student's interest in helping him. This also illustrated the degree of input and the conviction necessary on the part of a counselor for the preparation of clients for a family interview.

As the student began to reflect upon her role as a counselor here and the pattern of interviewing she was also able to conclude that it is difficult to shift from individual interviews to multiple ones. This served to confirm experience in other case situations leading to the conclusion that it often is easier to shift from multiple interviews to single ones rather than the reverse.

As this case progressed and Gregory kept testing the student, she continued to give much of herself in a consistent manner in view of the serious deprivations in this boy's life in order to enable Gregory to begin to view the world about him as less dangerous. She supported his need to express anger and differences. She emphasized his strengths such as his ability to show improvement in the classroom, and his likable personality. This had also been reinforced by his family, his classmates, his teacher, as well as his friend who participated in the first family interview. Thus, he was helped to feel more worthy as his self-image improved. The student concluded that Gregory reflects pervading difficulty of dealing with affection when she observed how agitated and anxious he became when concern was directed towards him. As he gradually continued to gain in self-confidence he became less fearful of the family interview in spite of continuing to raise some objections. This was his way of controlling the situation. The field instructor encouraged and supported the student in the use of family interviews in spite of Gregory's attempts at leaving the room, partially absenting himself from the interview in an effort to sabotage those interviews. With increased involvement in the interviews which followed, the family was beginning to show some cohesion. This encouraged the student to continue further in order to strengthen family focus with the use of family tasks which reinforced family cohesiveness. Interaction around such areas as tasks and responsibilities was used to develop clear communication, perception of self and others, and the effect of specific behavior on the family members.

At the same time, the student continued with individual interviews with Gregory at school in order to help him deal with the hostile aggressive behavior which deterred his involvement in family treatment. The student also continued seeing Miss M. whenever she permitted it in order to give her full support around her feelings of inadequacy and exploration of real need both she and the boys had for each other, thus enabling her to function more effectively and bring sustenance to this family.

This was a particularly difficult situation. The student, a bright, perceptive, and dedicated young woman, was aware of the frustrations she was experiencing in view of the serious limitations. In spite of the aunt's heroic effort to keep this family together, her own dependent needs prevented her providing a stable family base for these adolescent boys and a reactive chain had thus formed amongst them. There was some evidence that she may have been in competition with the boys' mother for her brother's affection, accounting for some of the hostility she may have felt towards the children.

Cases such as the above provide the field instructor with excellent opportunity to help the students through individual tutorial sessions, and group meetings to understand a family's functioning. By assessing the family dynamics, by understanding of and work with limited goals in a family situation, by learning how to involve all members of a family and by utilizing assistance from various members of a family as co-therapists, the student learns to use himself in a disciplined manner in the relationship.

The above student was very well aware of Gregory's struggle for his identity, the meaning of the entire mourning process for each of them, the roles of each member of the family, and the defenses used. She understood that the dysfunctioning in this family was present not only in the sibling system but also was related to the personality structure of the paternal aunt. It gave the field instructor the opportunity to consider with the student the differential use of single, joint and multiple interviews as necessary, to understand the operation of a family as a system, how to intervene in the circular interaction of a family and how to sensitize family members to the needs of each.

The results of student's attempt at family unit treatment thus far were clearly recorded by her as follows:

> Family unit treatment focused on shifting pressure from the 14 year old pulling family together around common concerns towards recognition that in a sharing process the family could prevent its disintegration. Treatment at this point has reduced stress on the 14 year old resulting in anxiety reduction and control over previous destructive behavior. Family tasks center on adjustment to new ideas and meeting parenting needs by simultaneously facilitating grief work.

**Teaching by Demonstration and the Use of
Critical Incidents in Field Teaching**

With a first year graduate student the responsibility of the field instructor is heightened since the field instructor additionally has to help with the theoretical underpinnings as a base for his practice. A parent-child problem assigned to the student served as a means of enabling the student to determine the rationale for family unit treatment, the meaning of interaction in the transactional system of the family, the handling of the interaction in using it to help the family members understand and deal with the effects of their behavior on each other, the parents' inconsistent handling of the children, the confusions this created, and the use of himself in the relationship with the family. This particular situation gave the field instructor the opportunity to teach the importance of dealing with interactional aspects in this situation rather than focusing on the underlying intra-psychic difficulties of the parents which could not and should not have been touched. Here the student was helped to understand that the basic social casework concepts are translatable to family treatment such as beginning where the client is and the importance of not proceeding at a faster pace than that for which the client is ready.

This family consisted of the parents in their late 30's, a son 12, and a daughter 9.

> The student was encouraged to examine the presenting problem, i.e., the behavioral difficulties of the 12 year old boy both at home and at school, including his smoking and truanting. Parents had used every form of discipline to no avail. They asked for advice in the area of parenting. The father also indicated some attention should be given to his wife since he perceived a great deal of the boy's acting out as a response to her rejection of him. In the initial two joint interviews, it became very clear from the history how tenuous was the father's adjustment, and how the mother's provocation resulted in marital discord and was spilling over into the intra-familial relationships. Both partners were using denial in order to retain the present state

of equilibrium which was disturbed by the boy's behavior causing the parents to look at their marriage. The mother's role as the disciplinarian had produced some conflict between her and her husband. When punishing the children, they would cry as the mother approached them, causing the father to believe that the mother was hitting them too hard. This was followed by an argument between the parents which produced a circular pattern in which the children manipulated the parents by provoking them into an argument and, thus, they removed the focus from themselves.

Through observation of the family in operation, and by listening, the student was helped to understand the transactional system, the family's mode of maintaining equilibrium and their characteristic coping mechanisms. In view of the father's marginal adjustment (he had a serious breakdown previously), student was helped to understand the importance of keeping this man's suspicions in relation to the mother encapsulated, and, therefore, family interviews were indicated. The family was able to see how each one was involved in the total problem and how when the first child improved the second one became worse. Together they were able to find solutions to the problem as they were helped to understand the effect of their current behavior on each other.

In another case situation the field instructor joined a second year graduate student in a family unit interview.

The family consisted of the parents, ages 39 and 37 respectively, and their four children, a son age 15, and three daughters ages 14, 12, and 9. The mother had previously applied at the agency for help in coping with behavioral difficulties of the son and older daughter. The father was described as a strict disciplinarian while the mother was more permissive and inconsistent in her handling of the children.

The last application was around the behavioral difficulties of the son. The student had several family interviews during the social study period during which time the son had shown considerable improvement but mother remained unhappy. The student discussed with the mother the need to understand the family as a unit. The family was prepared for this interview and the field instructor participated with the student in the interview by injecting leading questions, making observations and dealing with the here and now. Both the student and the field instructor saw clearly the father's tendency to remove himself from the interview, thus leaving the mother to deal with the children's complaints. The mother, a very insecure, anxious and depressed woman, had difficulty in her maternal and marital roles. This interview revealed how she abandoned her role as a mother, permitting the 14 year old daughter to take over, which served to reinforce the latter's need to isolate herself from her peers and become the mother person in relation to the siblings and, unconsciously, the spouse to her father. The struggle for her identity became clear. She disciplined the younger children, argued with her brother who enjoyed teasing his siblings, and at the same time was very angry with her mother around inappropriate limits the mother had set up for her in terms of dating and attending social events. Also evident were the double bind messages from the mother around socializing with her peers as the mother verbalized the need for the daughter to see her friends yet kept her occupied consistently with household chores. This daughter seemed to be the symptom bearer and was trying to make it very clear how pained she was.

At the same time, the 12 year old seemed to be very calm, composed and pseudo-mature. She seemed to have the right answers all the time, spoke well of the mother and father, letting them know what wonderful parents they were, and it was difficult to ascertain at first what the problem was since the 14 year old was obviously so annoyed with her. The mother was greatly encouraged by the words of the 12 year old, responded with praise, but the father constantly had to be involved for his reactions throughout the interview. As the field instructor recognized the pain of the 14 year old around the fact that she was actually complaining of having the responsibility of being a mother person in many respects without the authority that goes with it, she was freed sufficiently to explain how the 12 year old is constantly provoking her, using her clothes and other things without ever asking and shifting responsibility upon the 14 year old without giving her any help. In response to field instructor's comment that this appeared to be the responsibility of the mother and that a 14 year old was too young to carry this kind of responsibility, the rest of the family then each began sharing similar experiences and the father, too, was able to say that the 12 year old has been quite provocative with all of them and that one of these days she will get into serious trouble.

This was the first time the entire family was able to hear the complaints of the 14 year old clearly. The student was here helped to understand the family's operational system, the circular interaction that took place following which she was then able to arrive at a diagnosis and treatment plan with the family.

Another first year graduate student, a young married woman in her early twenties, had no social work experience in the field except some minimal social work orientation through past contacts with social workers. The student was bright, interested in social problems and had a youthful enthusiasm and idealism.

In this family situation, it became clear that the mother was controlling a latency age girl by limiting her activities, her freedom to play with other children on the basis that she was too young; yet she demanded adult behavior of her in relation to the responsibilities and chores in the household and care of younger children. As both parents were helped to develop awareness of this behavior, the student enabled them to examine their feelings surrounding it and to recognize the confusion the child experienced due to the conflicting directive given to the child. In addition, they were helped to see where they projected all of the problem on the identified client because that particular child reminded them of a relative of whom they had always been quite envious.

The use of a taped interview in field instruction is illustrated with the above-mentioned student who used the tape to enhance client's self-awareness.

The family had a very controlling mother who did not permit appropriate involvement in the family interviews by the family members. The student did not feel comfortable in confronting the mother with this. It was recognized in conference, that unless this was handled with the mother, the family would not be able to make any progress, even though there was recognition that the treatment goals were very limited. The field instructor had suggested the possibility of taping the interview and then playing it back to the family in the next interview as a means of giving the family a basis for self-observation. The field instructor afterwards listened to the taped interview together with the student. As a result, the mother's controlling behavior became more obvious to the student who, in turn, now was more convinced that playing the tape back for the family might be helpful. The interview revealed that the adolescent girl in this family had told the student that it was her feeling that these interviews were a waste of time because the parents were putting on "a good front" and the children did not feel free to express themselves. This served to reinforce the student's decision to use this tape with the family in the following interview. They listened very carefully, and she was very gratified to see the reaction of the mother who was the first to recognize her role in this family when she exclaimed, "My gosh, I'm the only one who's doing all the talking." When the student encouraged a closer examination of this, there was more communication on the part of the members of the family than there had been in the previous interviews. As the mother was able to recognize her role, she then began to control her verbal domination and the remaining members were freed to begin to participate more fully in subsequent interviews.

A first year graduate student, a young man in his early thirties, who had been practicing another human service profession prior to his social work education, had had a long standing concern for social problems. He was alert, flexible in his thinking and his personal values were basically identical with those of the social work profession.

The student came to the field instructor for help in dealing with a family situation. A mother had telephoned the office because of her 17 year old son's problems at school—truanting and under-achieving and finally expulsion from school. The mother was a very anxious, tense woman who

defended herself by constant chatter, overpower-
ing her husband, son and also the student.
She was over-protective yet very inconsistent in
her relationship with her son to whom she attached
herself and unconsciously ascribed to him the
role of the spouse. The student asked the field
instructor for help in reaching this mother and
also in involving the father in the planning.
The mother spoke for all of them. She would
call the student and keep him on the phone for
about an hour. The field instructor helped the
student to discourage this and instead to invite
the parents to come to the agency for interviews.

With the student's consent and appropriate preparation of the family, the field instructor decided
to sit in the interview with the student. The
mother indicated that she felt she had done
everything possible for the boy and flatly stated
that she will not change. She referred to the fact
that it is all her husband's fault and that he
will have to do something about it. He remained
passive in the interview as did the son. The
mother spoke at great length about the past and
did not permit examination of the current situation.

This interview was used in two ways. One, to teach
the student the role of the worker in a family situation
and two, to teach the student how to cope with resistance
which he encountered in this interview.

The student was also taught here how to focus an
interview on relevant problems and how to handle re-

sistance which produced therapeutic economy. The student used clues from the field instructor's handling of the interview, supported it, asked the family questions and reinforced the interventive techniques by his support of the family members, leaving them free to project whatever hostility they felt on the field instructor.

> In the initial phase of the interview it was pointed out that the field instructor was an outsider not a member of the family but the mother kept referring to the field instructor and the student to ask for advice and wanting the support from the counselors in relation to the opinions which she expressed. This was a maneuver on her part to make the field instructor part ·of the family and strike up a personal relationship. Recognizing this, the field instructor moved on to involve the husband in the interview by asking for his opinion.
> The mother tried to interrupt, bringing in unrelated material from the past, in order to avoid being confronted with the nature of her behavior. With acceptance and recognition of her feelings, the field instructor indicated that they came here to concentrate attention on what was going on in the family now so that we could see and deal with the problems as she, her husband, and son experienced them currently. We talked about how they handled problems in general and the field instructor and the student became the supporters and controllers in this situation. We recognized the difficult task, supported her efforts to try to change the situation involving them

more in telling us how. At first there was no mention of involvement of the husband and we, therefore, asked directly for his participation. The mother tried to answer but we insisted on her listening to the husband and in this respect we controlled the situation, suggesting that the student could see her alone in addition to the multiple interview so as to give her every opportunity to discuss this further, if she so wished. We also controlled the situation by preventing scatter of content into aspects of life that were irrelevant to the present situation by explaining that problems are worked out in the present not in the past. We asked questions to keep the couple from moving out of the present, supported their making their own decisions and evaluation of causes of problems as they saw it. With this they were able to see that communication between them was really lacking. The father spoke of giving up his attempts to talk to her because she never "shuts up" and no one can get "a word in edge-wise."[2]

The mother became insulted and asked why he had never told her this before. The father asked if she weren't aware of it. She responded that this was the first time he told her that. The father, at this point, confronted her further with this behavior and stated that both he and the son feel the same way about it. They were left with the one alternative and that is to absent themselves from the household from time to time whenever an opportunity presented itself. She then started to cry and the student and field instructor both helped her to understand that it is often difficult and painful to face oneself. From there on, the couple started to talk to each other and the extent of our verbal communication diminished as they learned to begin to communicate with each other.

In terms of the resistances met, the student was helped to understand (1) the mother's projection of the difficulties on the father; (2) the mother's effort to have the counselor take her side and build up a personal relationship; (3) the mother's statement that she will not change; and (4) the mother's manipulation in relation to appointments with the student.

Throughout the period of working with this family, the emphasis was on the interaction rather than on the intrapsychic aspects. The help given the student was to understand that we do not deal directly with the intrapsychic material because of the mother's lack of capacity for psychological insight. The mother's compulsive talk was seen as a major defense and as a character trait which could not readily respond to individual treatment.

After the student's initial moment of anxiety subsided, the student found himself comfortable in the interview with the field instructor since he was helped by being taught how to communicate with the couple. He was greatly encouraged by the field instructor's observations of this couple as he listened to field instructor's comments which reflected diagnostic agreement with his findings. Another important factor was that the student was left free and encouraged to participate in the interview as he saw fit. It is of interest to mention that we found the method of the field instructor participating in an interview with a student effective only in situations where a treatment relationship with the family already had been established by the student. Otherwise, the family may find it difficult to relate to two counselors in the initial phase of the counseling process.

Footnotes

[1] The unit was funded by an NIMH training grant (USPHS-NIMH, Family and Child Welfare Training Grant No. 5 TI-MH 10031). In addition to being a training site for social workers for the family and child welfare field of practice, the unit also had as two of its purposes (1) creating a teaching and study center for incorporating new emphases and practices in the field work curriculum integrated with their introduction in classroom teaching, and (2) the identification of curriculum content and methodology in teaching family diagnosis and treatment.

Planning for the training unit was arranged in cooperation with eight family agencies in the tri-county area of Metropolitan Detroit. These agencies represented the major social agencies in this geographic area, serving to repair, enhance and restore the social functioning of individuals and families. By virtue of their voluntary auspices, they had as one of their functions experimentation with innovations in service and practice to enhance the social functioning and mental health of the people in the communities they served. The directors of casework in these eight family and child welfare agencies were designated by their agency to constitute an advisory committee to plan for this training proposal. Later they agreed to serve as a nucleus for the continuing evaluation of this training project.

The unit, consisted of five students, a faculty field instructor and a secretary. It was initially located (1965-66) in the Down River Family Service in Wyandotte, Michigan—now called the Family and Neighborhood Services for Southern Wayne County. The faculty field instructor who implemented the study, also functioned and participated at Wayne State University School of Social Work as a faculty member teaching second year casework methods and was involved in other appropriate academic assignments. The agency's focus on family treatment, its high quality of practice, and the excellent cooperation of the entire staff created a professional climate conducive to learning, experimentation and freedom for creative teaching in this atmosphere.

In 1966-67, the unit was relocated at the Family Service of Metropolitan Detroit, Northwest District Office, because of geographical difficulties involved in the distance of the agency from the School. The unit was transferred to this agency which also had an active interest in studying this approach and was incorporating it into the agency's framework.

[2] See this type of mother as described in Wasserman, Sidney, Casework Treatment of the Neurotic Adolescent and the Compulsive Mother, **Social Casework,** November 1962, Vol. 43, No. 9.

References

Beatman, Frances L., "The Training and Preparation of Workers for Family Group Treatment," **Social Casework**, Vol. 56, No. 4, April 1964.

Leader, Arthur L., "Supervision and Consultation Through Observed Interviewing," **Social Casework**, Vol. 49, No. 5, May 1968, p. 288.

CHAPTER VIII

AN EVALUATIVE STUDY OF
STUDENT LEARNING OF
FAMILY COUNSELING [1]

Scope and Purpose of the Study

Although the literature on family diagnosis and treatment continues to increase in this field, very little on the subject has been researched. Relatively little has been written on teaching this approach in the classroom and the field.

The present study was initiated at Wayne State University School of Social Work, Social Case Work Sequence in the academic year of 1965-66 in connection with the work of a field work unit [2] emphasizing a family diagnosis and treatment approach.

The training unit provided the opportunity for enhancing the armamentarium for dealing with the vast range of human, social and emotional problems which clients bring to social agencies for resolution and for help in restoring and/or improving their social functioning. Therefore, an effort was made to determine: a) what kind of student did well in understanding and applying the family treatment approach in practice, and b) what implications the study's data indicated for future case work curriculum planning.

The training program in the unit emphasized all the normal expectations and curriculum content of a regular first or second year field work placement in a social agency. In addition it emphasized the incorporation of a family-focused approach as a part of the field curriculum for the students in the unit.

The field work unit built into its design of operation,

the planned introduction of opportunities for both first
and second year students to learn family diagnosis and
treatment approaches by direct instruction and observation. Both individual and group supervisory methods
were employed in the field teaching and opportunities
for observing family interviewing were also provided.
It was felt particularly important for optimal learning
to try to identify readiness factors for using such approaches as early as possible in the student's educational
experience. Such a unit was seen as serving as an important base for gathering material in a controlled
fashion on the introduction of such new content in
field teaching. This effort complemented the introduction
of such content in the classroom teaching in the school
and contributed to a broadened base for social work
operations in the field of services to individuals and
their families.

Major Focus and Objectives of the Training Unit

Our conceptual framework was eclectic. The focus of
the training unit and the area emphasized for studying
and training was the family-focused treatment approach
to the problems of social functioning of families as a
mental hygiene technique for ameliorating and resolving
both family problems and the effects of such problems on
all the family members.

The major educational objectives were to broaden the
training of social work students to greater sensitivity to
the role of the family unit as the unit of attention in
social work services. Special reference was made to
broadening the students' concentration on understanding
the interrelationships of individual and group behavior
and how the network of roles in the family affected individual functioning and vice versa.

While first and second year students were exposed in
their class experience in the case work method classes
to information concerning the functions of the family
and how the family was affected by the interactions in
the transactional system, this orientation was most heavily
emphasized in the second year methods courses. The
field experience of both first and second year students
reinforced these classroom emphases.

METHODOLOGY

Sample Selection

The subjects chosen for this study were full-time casework students pursuing their Master's Degree at Wayne
State University's Graduate School of Social Work.

The eighty-nine first year and forty-three second year
casework students were given the same case study to
read and respond to in September, 1965 (before test)
and again in June, 1966 (after test)—at the beginning
and the end of the 1965-1966 academic year. The
students' responses to the study's questionnaire were
grouped into the following five areas: 1) identification
of the problem; 2) causation of the problem; 3) the
worker s behavior in relation to the family; 4) the
worker's activity; and 5) the family's desires and motivation.

A random selection of half the first year students (45)
and half the second year students (22) then composed
the sample. For the specific purpose of evaluating the
effectiveness of the family counseling teaching model
(in the students' field experiences), an additional group
of five subjects was created consisting of students who
were placed in an agency where the family treatment

method was specifically being taught (Group A). This group raised the sample's total to seventy-two subjects (45 + 22 + 5).

Two comparative or contrast groups of five subjects each were then chosen from the original sample (of 67). The five subjects in Group B were selected from all those students placed in family agencies without a special orientation towards the family treatment approach. The five subjects in Group C were selected from all those subjects who were not placed in family agencies, and where the family treatment approach was not practiced.

Evaluation Process

For purposes of scoring the subjects' responses to the case study's questionnaire, a four-step process was developed. In stage one, three judges were recruited and assigned to independently isolate the range of student responses that would be acceptable answers in each of the five question areas. In pooling the judges' assignments, it was determined that there were a maximum of three (3) acceptable responses for Area I, five (5) for Area II, one (1) for Area III, four (4) for Area IV, and three (3) possible acceptable responses for question Area V.

In stage two, two "official judges" randomly selected three sets of responses (before and after tests) for a trial run—scoring these responses according to the number of acceptable responses for each area. These independently arrived at judgments were then compared and the judging techniques were refined and more clearly standardized.

In stage three, the official judges then independently scored the seventy-two response sets in the same manner as in stage two. Again, these quantitative scores were compared and mutually acceptable scores were established in the few instances where discrepancies existed.

In stage four, the judges independently and then jointly made qualitative evaluations of each subject's responses in each of the five question areas—using the previously arrived at quantitative scores as guidelines. A subject's response that was evaluated as "poor" was then given a score of 05 points, an "average" response was worth 10 points, an "above average" response was worth 15 points, and a "good" response was assigned the maximum 20 points.

These point scores thereby provided indices of where each student started in September 1965, where he ended up in June 1966; and hence, how much knowledge and development he acquired with respect to family treatment in theory and practice during the academic year. When comparing these scores with such background data as the subject's ages, sex, marital status, previous work experiences, etc., it was hoped that some of the characteristics and qualities of those students showing the greatest improvements could be ascertained. Finally, by controlling much of this background data, it was hoped that a comparison of Groups B and C with Group A (the family treatment unit) would give further direction and information regarding the specific benefits resulting from the family treatment model's approach to practice in the student's field work experiences.

RESULTS

In reviewing stage four of the evaluation process, it can readily be seen that a sixth area, the subjects' total case scores (TCS) could be created by adding together the case scores in the five question areas. Similarly, each subject's degree of improvement or decline (change variable) in his six case scores (including total case scores) could then be ascertained by subtracting his before test score from his after test score for any or all of the six question areas. The results which follow will highlight the subject's total case score (TCS) change variable for the analyses of trends and significant relationships.

This study found that the entire sample of seventy-two subjects averaged a gain of 5.08 points in their *Total Case Scores* (TCS) change variable. Twenty-one subjects declined in the Total Case Scores, eight subjects remained the same, and forty-three subjects (59% of sample) showed improvements in this change variable.

Comparing Total Case Score Changes/Background Data

The study found that the twenty-eight male subjects improved an average of 5.24 points on their Total Case Scores as compared to an average of +4.98 points for the forty-four female subjects ($p < .05$). Both sexes showed their greatest gains on change variable four, assessing the worker's activities ($p < .05$).

When the subjects' ages were compared to their T.C.S. changes, a negative relationship was found. Only the +5.17 points displayed by the youngest subjects (20-29 years) was above the sample's mean change, and significant at the .05 level. Again, all age groups showed the greatest improvements on variables four (worker's activities) and also three (worker's relationship with family).

It was also determined that the twenty-eight single subjects showed the greatest improvements in their T.C.S.'s as reflected in their 6.50 point average gain (p $<$.05). The thirty-six married subjects' averaged a gain of $+4.14$ points on their T.C.S.'s (p $<$.05). The divorced or separated subjects, however, showed in their average T.C.S. gains of $+3.75$ points, a considerably lower level of improvement than the $+5.08$ points shown for the entire sample's mean T.C.S. change.

The study also found that those subjects with prior work experience in social work, or in a related helping profession displayed average T.C.S. gains of 6.79 points (p$<$.01) and 5.52 points (p$<$.05), respectively. Those subjects having non-related or no prior work experience obtained total case score changes that averaged only $+1.25$ points and -2.50 points respectively—considerably below the sample's mean T.C.S. change of $+5.08$ points.

Related to the above results, was the finding that subjects with undergraduate majors in social work or the related social sciences showed T.C.S. changes that averaged above the sample's average ($+7.45$ and $+8.40$ points, respectively), whereas subjects with undergraduate majors in education, liberal arts, or religion showed gains in their T.C.S.'s that were below that of the entire sample. It was interesting to note, on the other hand, that no relationship was found between the subject's undergraduate grade point averages and their total case score movements. The greatest improvement ($+6.68$ points) was exhibited by those subjects having an undergraduate G.P.A. between 2.60 and 2.99 (p $<$ .01). All other subjects scored below the sample's mean T.C.S. change.

The study also indicated that those subjects being supervised, in their field work, by supervisors with at least four year's experience (in supervision) showed greater gains in their T.C.S.'s when compared to students with supervisors having fewer years of experience.

One of the more interesting results was the finding that the first year students averaged 7.94 points in their T.C.S. changes ($p < .01$), as compared to an actual decline in the second year students T.C.S.'s, averaging .85 points. This finding becomes the impetus for the short section (2) which will follow.

Finally, the study found no discernible trends relating the subject's T.C.S. changes to either their religious, occupational (of parents) or placement (where the student was placed for the academic year's field work experience) backgrounds.

Before closing this section, it would be valuable to make a final comment. Breaking the above results down further, in most instances, the subjects showed the greatest improvements in their case scores on variables three (worker's relationship with family) and four (worker's activity). The least improvements, and often times actual declines in case scores, were generally displayed on variable five (the family's desires and motivation).

Comparison of Total Case Score Changes/Class Level/ Background Data

When a more thorough investigation was initiated in order to better understand the large differences between the first and second year students' T.C.S. changes, one prominent trend was evident. In almost all instances, the first year students had considerably lower T.C.S.'s than the second year students on the before test, but were much closer (though still generally lower) to the second year students T.C.S.'s on the after test. Relatedly, when the background data was added to this brew, it was found that this same trend existed regardless of the kinds of groupings. Additionally, however, some very notable and enlightening information was also evidenced.

For example, the study found that male subjects improved on their T.C.S.'s in both their first and second years (although they displayed far greater gains during their first year), while the female subjects were less stable—with first year females showing the greatest gains in their total case scores(8.41 points), while second year females actually declined an average of −2.20 points in their total case scores.

Similarly, the older subjects (40-49 years age group) showed the greatest stability on their T.C.S. changes— as reflected in their first and second year scores. The first year subjects in this age group averaged 4.40 points as compared to a +3.34 points for second year students in this same age group. The younger subjects, on the other hand, showed larger gains in the T.C.S.'s when in their first year, but actually declined in these scores when in their second year (i.e., lesser stability).

When the sample was broken down by marital status, another interesting trend resulted. The single subjects were the least stable in their scores, obtaining the greatest gains in their T.C.S.'s while in their first year (+9.64 points), but also the greatest declines when in their second year (−5.00 points).

The study also found that those subjects having undergraduate majors in social work and/or prior work experiences in social work or in the related helping professions also displayed the greatest stability. The first year subjects in these categories achieved the greatest improvements in their T.C.S.'s, while the second year subjects in these groups were the only ones among all second year students to actually retain some positive movement in their T.C.S.'s.

A final interesting finding in this area was the result indicating that first year students obtained very similar

T.C.S. improvements regardless of their supervisors' years of field instruction experience, whereas this was not the case for second year students. While only two out of the twenty-four second year subjects had supervisors with less than four years of experience, these subjects averaged a decline in the total case scores of almost 17.00 points! The second year students having supervisors with at least four years of experience, on the other hand, averaged +.69 points on their T.C.S. changes.

Comparison of Total Case Score Changes/Groupings

It should be remembered that three groups (A, B & C) were created with five students each to compare the progress, shown by a group being exposed to family treatment in theory and practice (Group A) with two groups where either no special emphasis was placed on such a model in the student's field placement (Group B), or where such a model was not even permitted to be practiced in the placement (Group C). Table I shows the average Total Case Scores for Groups A, B & C, and the changes in T.C.S.'s for these groups.

TABLE I

COMPARISON OF TOTAL CASE SCORES, BY GROUPINGS

Case Score	GROUP A		
	Before Test	After Test	Change
Total Case Score	37.00 Points	47.00 Points	10.00 Points

Case Score	GROUP B		
	Before Test	After Test	Change
Total Case Score	38.20 Points	40.20 Points	2.00 Points

Case Score	GROUP C		
	Before Test	After Test	Change
Total Case Score	44.60 Points	47.00 Points	2.40 Points

It can be seen that the subjects in Group A (field work unit with special emphasis upon the family treatment model) showed greater improvements in their T.C.S.'s (+10.0 points) than did the subjects in Group B (+2.00 points) or Group C (+2.40 points).

In a two-way analysis of variance, some trends were abstracted which might also shed additional light upon the determination of what kinds of subjects (based upon their background data) might be best and/or least capable of benefiting from the family treatment model. For this reason, the results which follow will deal solely with those subjects in Group A (family emphasis unit). Statistical significance for the findings, however, was not obtainable because of the limited sample sizes (five subjects per group), and should be kept in mind while reviewing these findings.

In Group A (family emphasis unit), the male subjects averaged +12.50 point gains in the T.C.S.'s as compared to an average gain of +8.33 points for the female subjects. The male subjects also ended up with higher T.C.S.'s, as indicated by the after test.

For subjects in Group A, a positive relationship was found between their ages and the improvements displayed in their total case scores. The youngest group (20-29 years) gained an average of +8.33 points, as compared to +10.00 points for the middle age grouping (30-39 years) and +15.00 points for the older subjects (40-49 years). It might be recalled that, for the total sample, a negative relationship had been found between age and T.C.S.'s.

Similarly, despite the fact that all five subjects in Group A were married, and therefore no comparisons could be made within this single group, it was interesting to note that these married subjects showed the largest average gains in the T.C.S.'s when compared to the subjects in either of the other two groups, regardless of marital statuses. This, too, differed from the entire sample's results which showed the greatest gains being made by the single subjects.

As was true for the entire sample, however, the subjects in Group A who had prior work experience in social work or in a related helping profession, also showed the greatest average gains on their T.C.S.'s. As was also true for the sample, no clear relationship or conclusions could be drawn when the religious backgrounds of the subjects in Group A were compared to Total Case Scores. Finally, it was also noteworthy that while the T.C.S. changes for the subjects in Groups A, B, and C, when broken down by class level, also paralleled the total sample's results (i.e., first year improved considerably more than second year subjects), one interesting difference arose. Among the second year students, only those in Group A continued to display improvements in their Total Case Scores, whereas the second year subjects in both Groups B and C all averaged declines on their T.C.S.'s.

DISCUSSION

Part One

In this part of the discussion section, primary attention will be focused upon the determination of what kinds of students generally displayed the greatest improvements in their Total Case Scores during the academic year 1965-1966; and, more specifically, what kinds of students might be best suited for and most benefited from the family therapy treatment models' approach in their field work experiences. Accordingly, the findings for the entire sample will be evaluated, where relevant, in comparison with the findings for the subjects in Group A (family emphasis unit).

The study found that the male subjects in the sample improved more than the female subjects on their T.C.S.'s. This same condition existed for the subjects in Group A as well. One very likely reason for the males' better showing was that our sample indicated that the newer enrollees into the social work master's program were more often younger, and more often males. These newer enrollees were actually the first year students; and, as will be discussed in the second part of this section, there are several possible explanations for why the first year students did so much better than the second year students.

This same consideration very likely explains why a negative relationship was also found between the sample's ages, and the improvements displayed in the T.C.S.'s. Again, class level may dominate the students' learning potential. Another not altogether contradictory explanation may be the possibility that the older subject's Total Case Scores, particularly while in their first class year, were depressed by the readjustment to school routine and, perhaps, the unlearning of well-routinized work experiences that was demanded of them. On the other hand, the finding that a positive relationship existed between the ages of the subjects in Group A, and their T.C.S.'s may suggest the possibility that the older student may be better suited to the particularities of the family therapy method.

Since there is an acknowledged relationship between one's age and one's marital status, this would be the next place to look. For the entire sample, single subjects showed the greatest T.C.S. gains. This is again likely related to class levels and the negative relation found between T.C.S.'s and ages. As noted in the results section, however, the five married subjects in Group A displayed greater gains in the T.C.S.'s than any of the other subjects in either Groups B or C. This may suggest the possibility that the family therapy method was capable of benefiting all subjects regardless of their marital status— subsequently the Group A subjects T.C.S.'s were raised above the T.C.S.'s of subjects in either of the other two groups. It may also offer the possibility that married subjects are more receptive and attracted to such a method. These two possibilities are by no means mutually exclusive, and in fact might both have been operating.

This study also found that, for the entire sample as well as for Group A (family emphasis unit), those subjects who had social work or related helping profession prior work experiences showed greater gains in their T.C.S.'s than did subjects without such job experiences. Similarly, it was found that those subjects, in either the entire sample or Group A, who majored in either social work or the social sciences also scored greater gains in their T.C.S.'s than did those subjects with undergraduate majors in other fields. Both of these findings underline the values that one's previous exposure to social work, as a helping profession, might lend to one's learning and educational experiences while pursuing a higher degree in the field.

While no relationships were found when the subjects' religious and occupational backgrounds were compared to their Total Case Scores changes, one final finding appeared noteworthy. It was found that, in the entire sample, those subjects having field instructors with at least four years of field instruction experience obtained the greatest gains in their T.C.S.'s. In Group A, all five subjects had an instructor with at least four years of experience, and these subjects averaged greater improvements in their T.C.S.'s when compared to any of the other subjects in Groups B or C. These findings suggest that the instructor with the greater number of years of supervisory experience may be more helpful in the student's educational pursuits. The findings also suggest the possibility that the supervisor with a greater amount of experience may be more effective in slowing down or even reversing the tendency for second year students to perform so much more poorly than the first year student.

Part Two

In this section, attention will be focused upon a few of the possible explanations for the existing T.C.S. differences between first and second year students.

Probably one contributing factor was that the second year students were exposed to the added pressures of completing their research requirements; whereas the first year student had no such added burden. These pressures may have restricted the students' involvement in both their classroom and field work experiences—thereby and probably restricting their T.C.S.'s.

A second, more complex, issue involved the possibility that the first year students were being exposed to material in their class work (particularly) that was compatible with the study's questionnaire. Supportive of this explanation was the fact that all of the subjects generally did best on variables three and four (establishing a relationship—worker's relationship with the family—and the beginning differentiations between treatment approaches—worker's activity); which were first year class materials, and, which required an approach that was worker-centered rather than client-centered. An approach, in turn, which was more likely characteristic of the first year's emphasis.

A third explanation of the discrepancies that existed between first and second year students appeared to follow from the above considerations. It was quite probable that if the material required in the students' responses to the questionnaire was more relevant to first year's material, these questions were not valid indices of the students' knowledge of the family counseling approach (which, by the way, was not emphasized in class until the students' second year). Not having an opportunity to display in the tests the practical and theoretical knowledge that they had acquired regarding family treatment, the second year students' scores were perhaps diminished because of the unlearning or forgetting of the first year's material.

A fourth possibility, of course, may be that basically the second year's class content at that time (which emphasized family therapy in the fifth quarter) may have presented a discontinuity in content which affected the second year students' progress towards their educational goals. For some second year students a conflict might have existed between the second year students' class and field work experiences—whereby they were taught family treatment theory in class but faced limitations in its application in the field.

An analysis of the data adds one final explanation to these above considerations. This study did find that the greatest instability in T.C.S.'s (discrepancies between first and second year students) existed particularly for the younger, unmarried female. This would merit further investigation about possible relationship to this status.

149

IMPLICATIONS

One of the major questions that was raised in this study dealt with the large differences between the first and second year students' Total Case Score changes. Explanations as to why the second year students did so poorly included: the added pressures of completing a research requirement that was selectively inherent in the second year; and, the broader concern that the questionnaire just was not designed to measure the students' grasp and understanding of the family therapy method— but, was rather geared to the first year's course content and learning experiences.

The first explanation suggests the possibility that further research might consider a longitudinal study of two matched or contrasted groups where one group had a required research project, while the second group did not. With respect to matching these subjects, the question might first be raised as to what variables (besides those reported in this study) may affect the students' learning experiences as measured by any questionnaire. It would seem that the entire area of the emotional and professional relationship existing between instructor and student, in the field work setting, would have to be much more closely evaluated. Tapping this area would be a very difficult job. Conceivably, a major segment of a future study's energy would have to be devoted towards the construction of a valid and reliable ranking system or attitude survey for such purposes.

It should be recalled that the present study attempted to set up three contrast groups by which to identify the effectiveness of the family treatment model. It would appear that in view of the above considerations, such a design was premature. Assuming that the much needed larger samples (than five subjects for each group) were chosen, one's primary concern might be in choosing such samples randomly and first attempting to identify which variables required controls (to ascertain the effectiveness of any particular method) and which variables required no such controls.

A basic concern of this study was the possibility that the questionnaire was more oriented towards the first year's class and field work content than the second year's. As such, it had placed the second year students in the immediate disadvantage of a greater distance of exposure to such content.

Future studies, if they are to be interested in truly measuring the effectiveness of any treatment method, must be sure that their measuring instruments are valid and reliable. In the present study, it would appear that the instrument may not have provided the students with sufficient opportunity for displaying their knowledge of the family treatment model.

Footnotes

[1] Analysis of the data was prepared with the assistance of Michael S. Kolevzon, research assistant. Also cooperating in the planning and carrying out of this research were Richard English and Jacob I. Hurwitz as research consultants. Sandy G. Reid assisted in compiling the data and Marian Reavey and Florence White assisted in constructing the instrument.

[2] See Chapter VII, page 131 for description of the unit.

SECTION III

IMPLICATIONS FOR PROFESSIONAL EDUCATION

CHAPTER IX

ISSUES AND PROBLEMS IN
LEARNING, TEACHING, PREPARATION
OF CLASS AND FIELD TEACHERS,
AND CONSULTATION

Issues and Problems

As in all technical approaches to counseling, clarity is required about the theoretical base upon which one operates and this contributes to the counselor's ability to make differential use of different approaches in the counseling process. Also, the counselor has to be clear in his own mind about the relationship of the various treatment modalities including individual counseling, group counseling, family counseling, and the different theoretical models upon which such counseling is based as described earlier.

For example, in the family counseling process, one operates on the philosophical base that the family is the major procreative and socializing system in our society. When individual members of the family present maladaptive responses and problems, it is important to consider them not only in the light of the affected individual, but also in the light of the family milieu in which this occurs.

Since recent generations of family counselors have largely been trained in the various disciplines to understand and to work with individuals, some of the problems that arise in developing knowledge and skill in the family counseling approach are related to this orientation. Because of earlier concentration on the behavioral operations and functions of the individual, we frequently lost sight of the forest for the trees. Now, of course, the same can be said about losing sight of the trees in terms of looking at the family and its larger environment such as the neighborhood and the community. Since here we are concerned with the role of family counseling, we will focus mainly on skills and orientation required to understand the family and its functioning, and the approach that needs to be taken to understand and work with such dysfunctioning.

Another problem that arises in using the family-focused approach is the fact that theory and practice are often still far removed at this stage of development of the family-focused counseling approach. Therefore, though theoretically we may be developing conviction about the importance of a family focus, actual practice does not always support such a focus. Agencies, administratively and practice-wise, are sometimes still geared to focusing on the identified client rather than the situation in which the identified client is experiencing the maladaptive behavior and circumstances which bring him to our attention. To solve this problem, various research centers and experimental centers such as the Family Mental Health Institute of the Jewish Family Service of New York, the Palo Alto Mental Research Institute in California, and the Midwest Committee of FSAA on Family Diagnosis and Treatment have developed theory and new concepts basic to practice which need to be tested out and incorporated into practice approaches. As is true with all innovations, theoretical and otherwise, much time and effort needs to be expended on re-adapting our theoretical framework and practice approaches to such innovations. Hence, when training centers such as professional schools begin to teach new theoretical frameworks for practice there frequently is difficulty in coordinating didactic teaching in the school and the practicum which is more dependent on the treatment center, or the counseling center, for the implementation of new learnings, new methods, and the use of new theoretical formulations. Thus, one of the problems that very frequently confronts training centers and educational institutions has to do with this kind of discordance and discrepancy in the stages of development of innovations in practice and in theory. In order for such learnings to become available and practical, it is necessary for the practice centers to provide a hospitable environment for such innovations which includes encouragement for innovative thinking, doing and attitudes.

Another problem comes from habituation. All of us become naturally attached to methods which have proven useful, valuable and meaningful to us. If innovative concepts, formulations and practices become available, we need to deal with the problems of reorientation and adaptation that such innovative concepts and principles create for the practitioner.

As with all approaches in the counseling professions, we need to think not only of transference aspects, but also counter-transference aspects of the counselor's own attitudes, biases and experiences as they affect his readiness and ability to digest and absorb new concepts and practices. Also, there is the natural resistance to innovative ideas and practices based upon a desire to have confirmation by research and practice of the validity of new approaches.

It is perhaps most helpful to recognize that each innovation in a field like counseling has its place, if it has validity, and should take its place with all the treatment modalities already developed. With each new modality we must see how it fits and what its place is in relation to all the other modalities. However, we also have to think of this in a progressive sequence, namely, that as the different modalities are developed and found valuable and useful, we have to see how each relates to the other, what specific situations require, and which are most suitable. This will also depend both on the situation and on the orientation of the counselor. We have to recognize that the counselor must have considerable leeway in individualizing his approach to his clients.

We need to be aware of the fact that the counselor has to be given such leeway in following his own orientation. Many of the concepts and principles now enunciated and in use will need to be further validated by experience and controlled research.

Innovative counseling is not only a matter of professional education, but also related to continuing education and consultation. These efforts need to be in consonance with the family-focused counseling approach which would support the counselor's continuing efforts at developing and building the knowledge and skills required.

It has been pointed out that in all interpersonal relationships there is not only the manifest content, but also the latent content that we need to be concerned about, and which underlies ambivalences, confusions and distortions about the phenomena dealt with and the approaches used in treating the situation. Hence, when new concepts and theories are introduced they are subject to all of the ambivalence and distortion which any new phenomena may elicit. Consequently, in both the educational and practical application endeavors in family counseling, it is important to take such factors into account and to provide the counselor with the means for becoming aware of them and dealing with them.

Another area that requires our attention is that of continuing to develop the criteria for the differential use of family counseling approaches; for example, the importance of utilizing such an approach where the problems are manifested in relation to family role relationships and functional problems which are affected by and affect the transactional system of the family. In such situations, the behavior of the individuals involved are affected by and affect the family. Starting from these basic determining criteria, we elaborate the whole continuum of factors earlier described. Some of the factors related to the problems in the education and development of family-focused counselors are related to their own life experiences as well as the effects of being exposed to dysfunctional family situations with their demands, frictions and conflicts which may trigger counter-transference reactions on the basis of the counselor's own life experiences, biases and attitudes. These factors need to be recognized and dealt with in the development of the family counselor. It is important for such professional activities to be supported by continuing study, education, opportunities for staff development including ongoing development of skills, knowledge and means for keeping *au courant* with new developments in the knowledge and practice of family-focused counseling.

Content Versus Process

The family-focused counselor has a great deal to learn and develop in terms of recognizing the appropriate use of the content that he needs and acquires in his counseling with clients and families, and in his orientation to the ongoing process of the transactional system of the family. Though his responses and his interventions may be largely related to the process, he should never forego noting and taking into account facts that determine his emphasis on content or process which depends upon the ability, the state of maturity, the state of sophistication and the degree of conscious awareness which the clients have of their situations. On this basis he decides whether or not to emphasize content or process in his counseling.

The student, therefore, who has been educated in the school of thought which emphasizes content needs to develop greater awareness of the role of focusing on process and the interrelationship of content and process in family-focused counseling. He needs to learn where the focus should be largely on the social interaction and the social functioning, and where the content emphasis needs to be related to and properly oriented to the goal of affecting the process of the family's interactions and transactions. For example, it would be important when one is dealing largely with the behavioral responses of the family and their interactions, that the focus would, naturally, have to be on the process although the content would help to guide the interventions by the counselor.

Since the family-focused counseling approach is so heavily dependent upon and invested with the continuing knowledge that is being contributed from the social and behavioral sciences, continuing effort has to be made in this area to translate such knowledge into application in family counseling practice. And this, we believe, is one of the major areas for further effort and investment of resources that is needed in the development of the family-focused counseling approach since this would be the theoretical base which will eventually serve as the foundation for future development of this approach. Also, this underlines the need for continuing research and validation of both the theoretical basis for such an approach and the practical applications of such theory.

PREPARATION OF CLASS AND FIELD TEACHERS

It should be axiomatic that the professional school and the practicum should have wide areas of agreement on educational objectives and the theoretical framework employed in the educational process. Consequently, it is incumbent upon the professional school to be explicit and clear about the general theoretical framework taught at the school and how this should relate to the conceptual framework emphasized in the practicum in the field. This requires that there be continuing ongoing communication between the school and the field sites in order to keep abreast of changes and new theoretical emphases and conceptual frameworks used both in class and field. It is recognized that frequently the most significant gaps in the educational process exist, where they do, between class and field. It is, therefore, important that ongoing dialogue be characteristic of the interrelationships of these two important aspects of professional education. This requires spelling out concretely curricula and syllabi guiding educational objectives so that there may be a basis for checking the correlation and integration between these two important aspects of the professional training process.

One of the ways of insuring such integration and of fostering continuity and sequence in curricula is to have mutual responsibilities for the development and change of curricula, and through continuing dialogue to check the outcomes and the educational methodology used in order to achieve the agreed upon educational objectives. In relation to family-focused counseling which is our major concern, it is important that we be clear theoretically, semantically, and in practice as to the frame of reference. This requires clarity about definitions of terms, of concepts and also of functional operations. Common areas of confusion or disagreement need to be identified and constantly reduced to make the operation more functionally adapted to the needs of the students. Where both classroom and field teachers are involved in the educational process, it is, therefore, important that both have a common background in the theory of the practice as well as in the operations of the practice. Since this is one of the most frequent areas of difficulty experienced in training centers for counselors, it is important that we consider what are some of the ways that have been found to be effective for reducing gaps and misunderstandings between these two important elements in the professional educational process.

In the family-focused counseling approach, frequently questions are raised about whether this approach is feasible and appropriate for the great variety of settings in which the counseling process is carried on. It is the philosophy of the authors that the family-focused approach is not related to setting but rather to the clientele and their needs. As we have defined earlier, the family-focused approach is important wherever the problems presented by the clientele are either related to the family situation or affect the family situation. Therefore, in all of these circumstances, no matter where the clientele applies for counseling, this approach would have its place. Secondly, we need to be clear about what we mean by the family-focused approach, namely, as defined earlier that this involves an approach which focuses on the family milieu in which the individual either finds himself now, or has been related previously, and that this must be taken into account in the study, diagnostic and treatment process throughout.

As noted in the first section of this chapter, prior orientations may sometimes make it difficult for practitioners as well as teachers to change their theoretical orientation. It is incumbent upon the school and the practicum settings to offer staff development and faculty development activities such as institutes, professional workshops and ongoing consultation, formal classes and any other educational media for retooling and reorienting the earlier or prior orientation of the faculty involved in the educational process. This may require exposure of both class and field faculty to new methodologies in treatment with opportunity for testing these out in practice as well as in the teaching situation and research geared towards study and validation of such new methods. Also, comparative study of the relationship of the innovative methods and modalities in relation to earlier established modalities is needed. As in other treatment modalities, the family-focused counseling approach lends itself particularly well to observation either as participant observer therapist, or as observers behind a one-way screen or via mechanical means such as video tape. Here practice and education converge at the point of the innovation of new technologies. Experience with such innovations gives an opportunity to test out theoretical formulations underpinning such new modalities. Here again, we need to underline the importance in professional education of keeping a viable and ongoing line of communication and interaction between the class and the field, between theory and practice since professional discipline depends on this kind of interaction for its growth and development. It cannot be either totally dependent on theory or on practice, but must represent the optimal blend of the two. It is usually helpful, if clinical experience is available for faculty, in order to test out innovative treatment modalities.

CONSULTATION

Since family counseling involves the important and central social milieu in which the individual has his major growth and development during his life cycle, it is important that all sources of knowledge be made available to the practitioner. This would require consultation from a variety of disciplines including the scientific disciplines such as sociology, anthropology, social psychology, biology, physiology, etc., and also from the applied disciplines such as medicine, psychiatry, psychology, social work, education, etc. Such interdisciplinary functioning requires opportunities in the academic environment as well as in the clinical setting and the agency setting for such interchange. In the academic setting, this is somewhat more available in view of the great variety of disciplines and sciences which usually are involved in the structure of an academic setting. In the clinical setting in the agency, the number of disciplines available are usually more limited in scope and also more difficult to obtain. Also in clinical settings, usually one or the other discipline predominates in terms of control and, therefore, it is essential that the structure be such as to maximize the contributions of interdisciplinary efforts and functioning within whatever structure is predominant. This requires that the predominating discipline make use of not only other disciplines, but also of its own discipline. Thus, in the social agency, in addition to the utilization of consultants such as psychiatrists there should also be social work consultants, educational consultants and others who should be available to the staff in accordance with the requirements of their clinical situation. Consultation involves the free interchange of knowledge and clinical experience from all disciplines which includes self-determining usage of such contributions on the part of all disciplines involved. Thus, consultation could also be offered to and by private practitioners of family counseling, and includes not only consultation on clinical aspects of family counseling, but also continuing education activities for family counselors. Such consultation also would be helpful to other professions dealing with family aspects of functioning such as the law, medicine, education and nursing. In relation to the use of consultation in family counseling, this form of treatment is especially suited for consultation in the actual situation, so that a consultant could actually be brought in not only to observe but also to participate in the family counseling process as an educational and consultative device in order to help both the counselor and the clients cope with the situation which they are endeavoring to affect. This opportunity for direct teaching in the client-counselor situation is particularly available in this form of treatment since the same degree of confidentiality is not present in the family counseling situation where all the individuals involved are coping with the situation together more publicly, and therefore, are more available for direct intervention and involvement. Hence, the introduction of another therapist or consultant would be less of a threat to the counselor-client relationship than in individual counseling.

References

Ferber, Andrew S., M.D., and Marilyn Mendelsohn, MSW., "Training for Family Therapy and Family Interviewing at the Albert Einstein College of Medicine," Unpublished Paper, 1968.

Kempster, Stephen W., and Elias Savitsky, Training Family Therapists Through "Live" Supervision in **Expanding Theory and Practice in Family Therapy**, edited by Nathan W. Ackerman, M.D., Frances L. Beatman, and Sanford N. Sherman, F.S.A.A., New York, 1967.

Sherman, Sanford N., "Aspects of Family Interviewing Critical for Staff Training and Education," **Social Service Review**, Vol. 40, No. 3, September 1966, pp. 302-308.

CHAPTER X

STUDENTS' REACTIONS TO
LEARNING FAMILY COUNSELING

Thus far we have discussed at length what is involved in professional education and training for preparation for family counseling. Two reports follow, one by a first year graduate student and another by a second year graduate student of their experiences in learning family counseling and some of the issues and problems that they identified in this process.

The two students whose comments are cited below were graduate students of social work preparing for the Master of Social Work degree and had their practicum experience in a field unit specially focused on learning and teaching family counseling, and on identifying teaching method and curriculum content. (See footnote page 131) The comments by the students were prepared for presentation to an institute for field work instructors responsible for teaching in the practicum and for classroom teachers responsible for teaching theoretical content. The students' comments reflect their own theoretical orientation and illustrate the principles described in previous chapters. The following material was written by the students.

I.[1] Learning the Family Diagnosis and Treatment
Approach

Even though the emphasis of the unit in which I am placed is on family diagnosis and treatment, I want to say at the outset that this is not the only approach I am taught, but learned very early that this approach should be used differentially and have found that it often enriches the individual approach. Nevertheless, I have found the family unit approach more effective in dealing with certain families but have been experiencing mixed feeling toward it since, at first, I found it to be more difficult in relating to more than one individual at a time. It was very frightening and overwhelming to have four or five people sitting in my office at once. My initial discomfort at having to relate to more than one person at a time was increased when all the material I was receiving in the classroom was directed toward the individual approach. However, I have found that many of the concepts and techniques presented to me as a first year student have been applicable to the family approach, i.e., it has been emphasized in the classroom to work with the strengths of the individual and I have utilized this concept by working with the strengths of the individual and I have utilized this concept by working with the strengths of the family as a unit. However, it was necessary for me to receive most of my theoretical framework from my field placement.

As a beginner I found it most difficult for me to observe and pick up on the interactional process, and, consequently, my efforts with families was directed toward the individual within the milieu of the family group without first recognizing what the effect of each individual's behavior was having on the entire family unit. But once I could look at the interaction and relate to it I was helped to recognize the circularity of the interaction within the family unit which enabled me to understand the family as a system in operation. In some instances I could see how one member was reinforcing another member and, consequently, it was impossible to separate one individual from the total family pattern of operating. It became significant in treatment when the family members began to observe this pattern and what their contributions to it were.

As I gradually am becoming more comfortable with this approach I actually have very little difficulty in getting the whole family together and discovered that when I did make extra efforts to get everyone in, even though one member may feel he had no part in producing the imbalance, or when the parents felt they were having trouble only with one child and, therefore, not necessary to see the other children, it made them feel an important part of that family, e.g., the father, when in the past he may have felt otherwise.

I am certainly not saying that even when I was more comfortable with this approach there were results immediately. However, it has been my experience with families that I could get at the level of functioning more rapidly since I was relating to the interaction and the "here and now" which was taking place right in front of me, with the added advantage of having the whole family's perceptions and feelings rather than one or two individuals.

Not only did I find myself relating to the interaction but was surprised to realize that on a few occasions I was not only exploring the problems presented with awareness of the nature of the equilibrium or disequilibrium, but was relating to the basic unity and mutual interdependence of each member to each other and to the whole. This was, in fact, working with the strengths of the family which has led me to the conviction that no matter how disorganized the family may be in its appearance that there is nothing to work with, I have found that all the families I have come in contact with so far, which included a great deal of reaching out, did possess some positive feelings that contributed to an underlying basic unity of the family. And I would say that, since we all come from families, I could sense a demand on my part to be very aware of my feelings in working with these families in order to avoid taking sides in the relationship and remain neutral. This was clearly illustrated in my work with one of these families where this very borderline functioning individual of a suspicious character was able to relate to me when he recognized that I was trying to help the entire family and was not getting involved in his individual suspicions.

In my social study period I found it most helpful for diagnostic purposes to see the whole family at least once and to make a home visit. This enabled me to set up, together with the family, treatment goals and follow through on treatment plans. This finally leads me to the conclusion that the value of the family approach can increase the effectiveness of the worker and I personally feel comfortable and confident enough to continue using this approach.

II.[2]

Before relating to you my experiences with family unit treatment as a second year student, I would like to acknowledge that I will also be reflecting the thoughts and feelings of the other two second year students in the unit. They shared with me their own particular involvement with family treatment, and the material I will present is a composite of "our" thinking. I would also like to add that in some instances the difficulties I encountered are identical to those presented by Mr. Moore, but as much as possible I will try to differentiate them in light of second year learning.

My first year placement was in a psychiatric setting and during that time I had the opportunity to work with multiple family groups mainly for the purpose of gathering history on the identified patient or using family members as a backdrop for added understanding of that patient. In most of my active cases I intuitively felt that the use of the entire family in treatment would facilitate movement. The patient's problem was frequently a fear of communicating needs and feelings to the family which, given the supportive casework relationship, he was able to communicate to me. Although it was my role then to help him deal with the problems communicated, I often thought it would also be important for those closest to the patient to participate in his attempt at communication within the same supportive framework.

I can recall one instance where I did try reaching into the family of a suicidal, adolescent girl by seeing her and her parents but my treatment focus was primarily on my client, the girl. It was difficult for me to perceive the family, her parents and several siblings, as the client despite my awareness of the complex network of symbiotic relationships among them. At this point in my learning, I did have available to me the theory base with which to pull together the fragments of the family unit treatment but it was of little immediate utility. Because it was not systematically presented as part of the course plan, I saw it detached from the present development of my skills and as something I would learn later in my second year.

170

When I began this second year I anticipated difficulty in orienting myself to learning the family-focused approach as I had always heard that it was a process of "unlearning" the individual approach. This implied a loss of a method that was gradually, sometimes painfully acquired, and one that I was just beginning confidently to integrate into practice. At this point in the year I question whether viewing the practice of family treatment as "unlearning" makes the learning task more difficult. Isn't it really another treatment approach to expand and enrich our basic casework skills? As an added skill the use of family treatment gives me the opportunity to use treatment more differentially covering a wider range of client problems, and most important to offer the client more effective service.

My experience has been that the same fears and anxieties I brought to the learning of the individual approach apply to family treatment. The same uncertainty and experience of pain is involved in any intensive learning process. In some ways having a base of one-to-one casework skills facilitates the accommodation of the family approach once a coherent presentation of the theory is given. Individual dynamics and pathology have to be understood for the interactional family processes to acquire meaning, and the principles of establishing the casework relationship apply to securing the involvement of individual family members.

I would like now to describe some of the problems I have encountered and the techniques I have acquired in the practice of family treatment. Beginning with the social study phase with the client, I believe it is necessary to have at least one total family interview or home call in order diagnostically to determine the most effec-

171

tive treatment approach. Unless a clear family perspective is obtained, I don't think the choice of one-to-one treatment can be validly made as the transactional processes within the family may be the primary contributor to individual pathology.

When I first determined the use of family unit treatment for one of my cases and began interviewing, I had the same difficulties of my first year in relating to the total family interaction. What I observed was a group of separate individuals communicating their own separate needs and problems. I was unable to help them connect these unmet needs with each other and have them perceive the problems as belonging to the total family. I was uncertain of what my casework role was, and the frustration I felt was a fear of losing control over the interviews. I think my learning experience differed from Mr. Moore's because I was acquiring the theory base at the classroom level while also receiving field supervision that corresponded to my learning. In practice I have gradually been able to understand the nature of family interaction and relate myself more effectively to it.

Another difficulty in the use of family treatment is securing a contract from the family for this kind of approach. Often the primary client is the person being scapegoated by the family, and the investment in maintaining this particular kind of complementarity resists any threat of change. I have found that by addressing myself to all the members' need for a sense of family unity has facilitated the willingness of the family to become involved in treatment. From the time this commitment is made, I think one of the most important assets of family unit treatment is that much of the usual caseworker's role is assumed by the family itself.

Family members do the work of sustaining casework techniques, giving support to strengths and accepting feelings. Particular members attempt to improve communication by clarification and interpretation of their own and each other's statements. This kind of process is used in families with a great deal of strengths. I have met with situations where I have used a variety of treatment methods, by seeing parents conjointly and the children individually or multiply—as was diagnostically indicated. With family treatment I have also discovered that the definition of who in the family can be included can be viewed quite flexibly. Those persons who can be included in interviews do not have to be limited to the nuclear family but may extend over generational boundaries and even occasionally incorporate those people influential in the family's day-to-day living, like friends and neighbors.

In concluding my presentation I would like to address myself to the importance those who teach and supervise us have in facilitating the learning of family treatment. In any learning process there is resistance and anxiety on the part of the student, and those who educate us must have worked out their own doubts and resistances to family unit treatment before our anxieties can be effectively relieved and our motivation stimulated. The same kind of support the school and field offers the student in the learning of individual techniques is necessary to sustain our motivation through the regressions and plateau periods of family treatment. I think what has been most important to me is the strong sense of conviction in the strengths of this approach both in the classroom and my particular field placement. My experience has been that this conviction does not rigidly exclude other approaches but when family treatment is diagnostically indicated, then it should be used.

In the same way, the extent to which family treatment is used is determined by the agency's commitment to it. If the school encourages the development of this conviction in its students then at graduation we carry it with us as one of the expectations we have of the agencies for which we work. I am not certain how much of an impact graduates have had in practicing family treatment and what conflict it has created in agencies. However, if conflict has arisen then I think it appropriate to ask how much communication has there been between the school and agencies around the commitment to family unit treatment.

Footnotes

1. Lloyd Moore and Susan Nakell. Mr. Moore submitted I, page 166, and Miss Nakell submitted II, which follows, both using the same subtitle.

2. loc cit. page 169

CHAPTER XI

SUMMARY OF IMPLICATIONS
FOR PROFESSIONAL EDUCATION

The renewed interest in the social functioning of clients in social work and in the family counseling field as a whole is in consonance with the family counseling approach and the emphasis on the family as the unit of attention. Dealing with the family group as a unit of attention enables the counselor to view more dramatically and completely the impact of social forces on the family as a group rather than focusing on its segmented parts. A more comprehensive diagnostic base for the treatment of choice is offered.

Essential for teaching family counseling are (1) conviction about the theoretical and conceptual framework underlying this approach; (2) early exposure of students to this approach in the initial phases of their professional education program; (3) focus on the role of the worker in relation to the family group and the individuals comprising the family unit in developing professional discipline and self-awareness on the part of the student; (4) use of a variety of methods of instruction in class and field including live supervision, or active participation, by the instructor in the interviewing situation; (5) opportunity to observe such treatment methods in use in order to facilitate learning and diminution of anxiety and of student hesitance to extending his activity in behalf of more than single individuals; (6) opportunity to utilize family interviews to develop recognition of the role of the clients in carrying co-therapist responsibilities; (7) recognition of the need to focus on process as well as content in family counseling.

SECTION IV

SUMMARY OF CONTENT

CHAPTER XII

A SUMMARY OF CONTENT IN
OUTLINE FORM

SECTION I - Family Theory and Social

Work Practice

CHAPTER I - The Dynamic Role of Family Counseling in Enhancing Social Functioning: Its place in the Armamentarium of Social Work Treatment Approaches

A. The family is the basic social unit in society.

B. Family counseling aims to restore impaired functioning, to support current functioning and/or strengthen social functioning via removal of obstacles, resolution of conflict, by improving division of labor, by facilitating the meeting of basic needs of the family members.

C. Where appropriate, it supplements and/or substitutes for other approaches such as individual and other group methods.

CHAPTER II - Historical Development of Family Counseling

CHAPTER III - Cont'd

A. Theoretical underpinnings for an eclectic approach

   1. Psychoanalytic theory and ego psychology

   2. Transactional theory

   3. Communication theory

   4. System theory

   5. Field theory

   6. Small group theory

   7. Socio-Behavioral theory - extinction and reinforcement

   8. Socio-psychological - (Norman Bell)

   9. Principle of pervasivness of the Family Disturbance - Principle of indeterminacy (Pollak)
     Social role theory (Perlman, Hollis, Parsons and Bales, Spiegel)

  10. Assumptions underlying family treatment - (Pollak)

B. Semantics and Terminology

   1. Family-centered or oriented case work

   2. Family-focused

   3. Family unit diagnosis and treatment (Sherman - Bowen)

   4. Need response and feeling tendencies (Pollak)

   5. Family as a social system and sub-systems (Pollak)

CHAPTER III - Cont'd

   6. Homeostasis - equilibrium (System theory)

   7. Transactions and interactions (Grinker)

   8. Feed back - cybernetics - communication

   9. Family process

  10. Functions of the family

  11. Family compared with individual treatment

  12. Socio-psychological concepts (Norman Bell)

C. Schools of Thought of Family Treatment

     An eclectic approach to family treatment

   1. Psychoanalytic - conflict resolution - ego psychology - (Ackerman, et. al.)

   2. Communication theory (Satir et. al., Palo Alto School)

   3. Transactional School - (Grinker, et. al.)

   4. System theory (Pollak)

   5. Midwest Committee (Pollak) - Need response, values, goals, roles, communication patterns

   6. Field theory (Lewin)

   7. Small group theory - (Grace Coyle - Bardill and Ryan, Mary Louise Somers)

   8. Socio-behavioral - (Thomas, et. al.)

   9. Social role theory - (Parsons and Bales, John P. Spiegel and Frances Kluckhohn)

CHAPTER IV - Application to Social Casework Practice

A. Generic Application of Family Theory

Diagnostic and Treatment Approach to Social Casework Practice - Fields of Practice

1. Family and marriage Counseling

2. School Social Work

3. Social casework practice in health settings (medical and psychiatric)

4. Child welfare (substitute parental care, institutional care, corrections)

5. Adult corrections

6. Aging

7. Private practice

B. Issues in Family Counseling

1. Eclectic versus a unidirectional theoretical approach

2. Differential diagnostic and treatment approaches to the family

a. as a unit

b. as a series of sub-systems (spouse, parent-child, and siblings)

c. conjoint (parents re marital aspects)

d. multiple (more than one person at a time)

CHAPTER IV - Cont'd

    e. dyadic (one person at a time)

  3. Criteria for

    a. individual counseling

    b. family counseling

  4. Family counseling as a total process of study, diagnosis and treatment

  5. Content versus process emphases

  6. Need for administrative support and an adequate theoretical framework

SECTION II - Teaching Family Counseling

CHAPTER V - Orienting the Social Casework Student to the Family Counseling Approach

A. Need for early orientation in the professional educational process as related to social realities of family life, neighborhood and community aspects, agency, etc.

  1. Incorporation of family and individual models of study diagnosis and treatment

  2. A psychosocial approach (total Gestalt of bio-socio-psychological approach)

B. Importance of a hospitable practicum milieu to this approach

CHAPTER V - Cont'd

C. Developing a perspective regarding the relationship of individual and multiple approaches.

   1. Didactic - lecture, literature, case records

   2. Participatory-like role playing or participant observation

D. Relationship and transference aspects of client and counselor roles.

   1. Observation (verbal and non-verbal cues)

   2. Communication patterns

   3. Social roles in the transactional system

   4. Social goals and values of the family

   5. Interactional aspects and focus on interaction

   6. Transference aspects, cross transferences - (inter-generational and generational); counter-transference

   7. Therapeutic roles carried by members of the family

E. Role of the family counselor

   1. As an activator and enabler

   2. As a reflector

   3. As a resource person

   4. As a model of communication and behavior

CHAPTER V - Cont'd

    5. As a source of support

F. Methods of recording

    1. Written (process or summary)

    2. Audio-visual

        a. tape recording

        b. videotape

CHAPTER VI - Didactic Teaching in the Classroom

A. Theoretical Framework

    1. Eclectic approach drawing on all schools of thought

    2. Family theory based on

        a. socio-psychological (socio-cultural, social behavioral, psychoanalytic, ego psychology)

        b. systems approach

        c. transactional theory

        d. communication theory - field theory-cybernetics - information theory

        e. social role theory

        f. small group theory

B. Process of Family Counseling

    1. A more active participatory form of counseling in which clients and counselor each take an active

CHAPTER VI - Cont'd

role in observing, understanding and responding to the transactional relationships in the family.

2. Both intra - and interpersonal relationships are the media for the treatment process.

3. Focus is on social interaction.

4. Family diagnosis is based on these observations and is arrived at in a shared process between clients and counselor. The treatment contract is based on such participatory activity. Family diagnosis takes into account the individual's circumstances as they related to those of the other family members.

   Focus, observation, assessment of meaning of interactions and communication patterns, of goals, of values, of need responses, and of social role performance comprise the diagnostic process.

5. Family counseling is an enabling process which aims to activate and maximize the potential for social functioning of the family unit in behalf of its members and of the unit as a whole. It also aims to re-establish a state of equilibrium in the family's functioning.

CHAPTER VI - Cont'd

   6. Diagnosis and treatment are concurrent parts of the family counseling process; treatment begins when the clients decide to seek it and make their first overtures. Hence, each develops in a reciprocal relationship as a part of the total counseling process.

   7. Prognostic and evaluatory processes involve the use of research methodology in assessing and predicting outcomes.

C. Methods of Family Counseling

   1. Interviewing skills require some of the same ingredients as in the one-to-one, dyadic forms of counseling, e.g., purposeful use of relationship, acceptance, controlled emotional involvement, confidentiality, non-moralistic attitude, self-determination, self-awareness, self-discipline (Biestek) plus the use of knowledge of small group theory operative in multiple interviewing situations; such as about social role performance, social interactional phenomena, individual and group identifications, values and goals of the family group, sociocultural background, generational and inter-generational interaction, communication patterns, need

CHAPTER VI - Cont'd

  responses and fulfillment. The need for both office and home visits, and collateral contacts, and for reaching out to hard-core, multiple-problem, or diffident clients are taught.

2. Main focus is on social interactions rather than on client-worker interaction to help demonstrate to the family the relationship between the family interaction and the problem.

3. Focus and work with family strengths and potentials

4. The family unit is the client.

5. The family is viewed as a social system, the sum of which is greater than its parts.

6. Need to determine its distinct mode of operations as seen first-hand in its characteristic interactional process

7. The emphasis is concurrently on content and process as integral components of the transactional system in the counseling process.

8. Use of a generic pool of knowledge to describe and understand the unique operation of the family, its purposes and goals for itself, and relations to society

CHAPTER VI - Cont'd

9. Help family alter communication modes among family members.

10. Help family members understand the nature of family tasks and the problems in dealing with them, as well as their coping ability. Help and support victimized members, and get universal participation without fear of retaliation.

11. Help family members understand their current alignments and roles and how these affect the family operation.

12. Break into destructive agreements between family members and encourage the constructive agreements.

13. Establish and/or reinforce appropriate goals for family development, growth, stability in relation to the family tasks. At a given time, to help change inappropriate ones, goals for family development can be set up.

14. Effect change where defenses of family members are sufficiently flexible.

15. To increase the observing ego of the family members by increasing their ability to perceive the

CHAPTER VI - Cont'd

needs of others, and to observe their own be-havior and the responses they elicit

16. Help action-oriented families experience feelings and action together.

17. Teaching prognosis regarding treatability based on client motivation and opportunity and capacity to change.

18. Criteria for use of different types of treatment modalities

19. Role of the counselor in family counseling

    a. to be objective

    b. to be empathetic

    c. to observe, listen and respond to the family unit, all need to be taught.

20. Structuring a basis for family counseling

21. Need to distinguish between intrapsychic and interactional bases for family interaction

22. Developing students' tolerance for family inter-action by gradual exposure, immersion and par-ticipant observation in family counseling by others, role playing, videotapes, one-way mirror obser-vation, case records, lectures, discussion, litera-ture, etc.

CHAPTER VII - Practicum

A. Field work as a basic ingredient of professional education in:

1. Integrating class and field teaching as a means of translating theory into practice

2. In using the conceptualization of practice presented in class and in underpinning via field practice by putting knowledge to use

3. In an eclectic framework for practice

4. In teaching a threefold focus on family, the problems and the method of extending help

5. In focus on the transactional system and the interactional processes with concentration on the effects of maladjustive behavior followed by subsequent consideration of causal relationships, what, how, and why

6. By student movement from random action orientation to examination of stress presented in intake, exploration of current situation and how it relates to the past and intervention in current interaction

7. By student being taught his role in family counseling. Any personal problems in the student

CHAPTER VII - Cont'd

which serve as obstacles and need to be modified require treatment elsewhere if they do not respond to didactic instruction in class and field.

B. Progress of practicum - The field teacher instructs the student in how to put knowledge to use by:

1. Observing the family as an operational unit.

2. Listening with a purpose.

3. Understanding the meaning of the behavior and expanding his conceptualizations of the process

4. Responding to the family members' interaction in order

   a. to establish a treatment contract

   b. to open channels of communication

   c. to perceive the effects of his behavior on others and others on each other and himself

   d. to learn the ingredients of a relationship with a family

   e. to learn how to assess a family situation

   f. to learn how to intervene in order to enhance the functional capacities

   g. to learn how to maintain a relationship

   h. to learn how to determine when the family is

CHAPTER VII - Cont'd

ready to take over its own operations and to prepare for termination of the contract.

i. to learn how to evaluate the outcome.

j. to learn the differential uses of family counseling and its relationship to other treatment modalities

C. Method of field teaching in the practicum

1. Field teaching entails:

a. orientation of the student to

(1) community

(2) agency and its auspices

(3) clientele

(4) family and counseling process

b. exposure to agency practice via

(1) opportunities to observe agency practice

(2) appropriate work assignments

(3) individual and group conferences with a field instructor

(4) involvement in ongoing agency business such as staff meetings, committees, community contacts, etc.

c. helping the student conceptualize his practice

CHAPTER VII - Cont'd

or learn by thinking and feeling

(1) by observation

(2) by recording (tapes, video and written)

(3) by discussion (tutorial and group)

(4) by testing out knowledge base learned in class and stimulating further review of the literature

(5) role playing

(6) by direct guidance through "live" supervision in the counseling process

(7) by expanding the student's ability to operate by foresight rather than by hindsight

d. helping the student learn by doing via

(1) immersion in agency practice by case assignments

(2) engulfing him in the process of assessment, planning and participating in the family interaction in the interviewing situation in the office, in the home or wherever else the clients are

(3) teaching criteria for the differential use of treatment modalities

CHAPTER VII - Cont'd

2. What the teacher does

   a. the teacher is a mentor, guide, resource person, and evaluator of the educational process.

   b. the teacher serves as the liaison between the agency and the student in providing an appropriate educational experience by:

      (1) setting the pace and the climate for learning in accordance with the student's background and needs

      (2) helping integrate the student into the field setting and its culture

      (3) teaching the student the continuity of the study, diagnosis and treatment processes

      (4) helping the student learn the skill and techniques required to relate to a family

         (a) how to prepare a family for an inter-view

         (b) how one relates to a family from a therapeutically neutral stance

         (c) how to involve all members of a family as well as differential use of dyadic and other forms of multiple

CHAPTER VII - Cont'd

interviews

(d) how to focus on interaction

(e) how to recognize and deal with circular, repetitive behavior

(f) how to help the family arrive at agreement on goals and a treatment contract

(g) how to assess progress and readiness for termination and how to terminate

(h) teaching the student how to evaluate his service and student's learning and functioning

CHAPTER VIII - An Evaluative Study of Student Learning of Family Counseling

SECTION III — Implications for Professional Education

CHAPTER IX - Issues and Problems in Learning, Teaching, Preparation of Class and Field Teachers, Consultation

A. Issues and Problems

1. Family counseling requires a theoretical base and conviction by the counselor of the differential uses of family counseling and its relationship to other

CHAPTER IX - Cont'd

   treatment modalities such as individual and group counseling. Changes in the philosophy and theoretical framework from a concentration on dyadic as contrasted with multiple and family approaches.

2. If practiced in an agency setting, administrative support and provision is required as in other treatment modalities.

3. Anxieties regarding meeting with a family and being exposed to the demands, frictions and conflicts of a family situation will be related to their own experiences and ways of dealing with such circumstances and need to be dealt with in the educational process.

4. As in other forms of professional service it is important for students to have ongoing opportunity for shared learning about new developments in the field within and outside of the field work setting.

5. Content versus process

6. Additional and growing knowledge base from the Social Sciences

7. Need for research

CHAPTER IX - Cont'd

B. Preparation of Class and Field Teachers

    1. School needs to have faculty who are appropriately oriented.

    2. For field teachers who are agency based, knowledge regarding family counseling is needed, and school may have to provide opportunities for tooling up.

C. Consultation

    1. Need for social work consultation regarding social functioning aspects of family counseling process

    2. To private practitioners

    3. To agencies as a continuing education function

    4. Consultation to other professions such as law, education, and medicine

CHAPTER X - Students' Reactions to Learning Family Counseling

CHAPTER XI - Summary

    SECTION IV — Summary of Content

CHAPTER XII - Summary of Content in Outline Form

BIBLIOGRAPHY

TOPICAL BIBLIOGRAPHY [1]

Family Diagnosis and Treatment:
Theoretical

Ackerman, Nathan, "Family Psychotherapy Today: Some Areas of Controversy," *Comprehensive Psychiatry*, Vol. 7, October 1966, pp. 375-388.

Ackerman, Nathan, M.D., and Marjorie Behrens, M.A., "The Family Approach and Levels of Intervention," *American Journal of Psychotherapy*, Vol. 22, 1968, pp. 5-15.

Beatman, Frances L., *et al*, "Current Issues in Family Treatment," *Social Casework*, Vol. 47, No. 2, February 1966, pp. 75-81.

Borke, Helene, "The Communication of Intent—A Systematic Approach to the Observation of Family Interaction," *Human Relations*, Vol. 20, No. 1, 1967, pp. 13-28.

Boszormenyi-Nagy, Ivan, "From Family Therapy to a Psychology of Relationships: Fictions of the Individual and Fictions of the Family," *Comprehensive Psychiatry*, Vol. 7, 1966, pp. 408-423.

Boszormenyi-Nagy, Ivan, M.D. and James Framo (editors), *Intensive Family Therapy*, New York, Harper and Row, 1965.

Bowen, Murray, "The Use of Family Theory in Clinical Practice," *Comprehensive Psychiatry*, Vol. 7, October 1966, pp. 345-374.

Deutsch, Danica, "Family Therapy and Family Life Style," *Journal of Individual Psychology*, Vol. 23, No. 2, 1967, pp. 217-223.

Devis, Donald A., "Four Useful Concepts for Family Diagnosis and Treatment," *Social Work*, Vol. 12, No. 3, July 1967, pp. 18-27.

Feldman, Frances L. and Frances H. Scherz, *Family Social Welfare: Helping Troubled Families*, New York, Atherton Press, 1967.

Ferreira, A. J., "Family Myths: The Covert Rules of the Relationship," *Confinia Psychiatry*, Vol. 8, 1965, pp. 15-20.

Fleck, Stephen, "An Approach to Family Pathology," *Comprehensive Psychiatry*, Vol. 7, October 1966, pp. 307-319.

Group for the Advancement of Psychiatry, *Integration and Conflict in Family Behavior - Report #27A*, New York, GAP, 1968.

Hader, Marvin, "The Importance of Grandparents in Family Life," *Family Process*, Vol. 4, No. 2, 1965, pp. 228-238.

Hill, William G., "The Family as Treatment Unit: Different Techniques and Procedures," *Social Work*, Vol. 11, No. 2, April 1966, pp. 62-68.

Jackson, Don D., "The Study of the Family," *Family Process*, Vol. 4, No. 1, March 1965, pp. 1-20.

Kantor, Robert E. and Lynn Hoffman, "Brechtian Theater as a Model for Conjoint Family Therapy," *Family Process*, Vol. 5, No. 2, 1966, pp. 218-229.

Kempler, Walter, M.D., "Experiential Family Therapy," *International Journal of Group Psychotherapy*, Vol. 15, 1965, pp. 57-71.

Kempler, Walter, M.D., "Experiential Psychotherapy with Families," *Family Process*, Vol. 7, No. 1, March 1968, pp. 88-99.

Krapt, E. E., "Family Mental Health and the Older Generation," *WHO Public Health Papers*, Vol. 28, 1965, pp. 90-94.

Maruyama, Magoroh, "Monopolarization, Family and Individuality," *Psychiatric Quarterly*, Vol. 40, No. 1, 1966, pp. 133-149.

Mendell, David, M.D., Sidney E. Cleveland, Ph.D., and Seymour Fisher, Ph.D., "A Five Generation Family Theme," *Family Process*, Vol. 7, No. 1, March 1968, pp. 126-132.

Mottola, William C., "Family Therapy: A Review," *Psychotherapy: Theory, Research and Practice*, Vol. 4, No. 3, August 1967, pp. 116-122.

Murrell, Stanley M., and James G. Stachowiak, "The Family Group: Development, Structure, and Therapy," *Journal of Marriage and Family*, Vol. 27, No. 1, February 1965, pp. 13-18.

Nye, F. Ivan and Felix Berado (ed.), *Emerging Conceptual Frameworks in Family Analysis*, New York, The MacMillan Co., 1966.

Perlmutter, Morton *et al*, "Family Diagnosis and Therapy Using Videotape Playback," *American Journal of Orthopsychiatry*, Vol. 37, No. 5, October 1967, pp. 900-905.

Pollak, Otto, "The Outlook for the American Family," *Journal of Marriage and Family*, Vol. 29, No. 1, February 1967.

Rahoff, Vivian, John J. Sigal and Nathan B. Epstein, "Working-Through in Conjoint Family Therapy," *American Journal of Psychotherapy*, Vol. 21, 1967, pp. 782-790.

Rothbart, Mary K. and Eleanor E. Maccoby, "Parents' Differential Reactions to Sons and Daughters," *Journal of Personality and Social Psychology*, Vol. 4, No. 3, September 1966, pp. 237-243.

Safer, Daniel J., "Conjoint Play Therapy for the Young Child and His Parent," *Archives of General Psychiatry*, Vol. 13, October 1965, pp. 320-326.

Satir, Virginia, "Family Systems and Approaches to Family Therapy," *Journal of the Fort Logan Mental Health Center*, Vol. 4, No. 2, 1967, pp. 81-93.

Satir, V. M., "The Family as Treatment Unit," *Confinia Psychiatry*, Vol. 8, 1965, pp. 37-42.

Scherz, Frances H., "Family Treatment Concepts," *Social Casework*, Vol. 47, No. 4, April 1966, pp. 234-240.

Sherman, Murray H., Nathan Ackerman, Sanford N. Sherman, and Celia Mitchell, "Non-Verbal Cues in Family Therapy," *Family Process*, Vol. 4, No. 1, March 1965, pp. 133-162.

Sherman, Sanford, "Intergenerational Discontinuity and Therapy of the Family," *Social Casework*, Vol. 48, No. 4, April 1967, pp. 216-221.

Sigal, John J., Ph.D., Vivian Rahoff, and Nathan B. Epstein, "Indicators of Therapeutic Outcome in Conjoint Family Therapy," *Family Process*, Vol. 6, No. 2, September 1967, pp. 215-226.

Sprey, Jetse, "Family Disorganization: Toward a Conceptual Clarification," *Journal of Marriage and Family*, Vol. 28, No. 4, 1966, pp. 398-406.

Strean, Herbert S., "A Family Therapist Looks at Little Hans," *Family Process*, Vol. 6, No. 2, September 1967, pp. 227-234.

Tharp, Roland G., and Gerald D. Otis, "Toward a Theory for Therapeutic Intervention in Families," *Journal of Consulting Psychology*, Vol. 30, No. 5, 1966, pp. 426-434.

Vincent, Clark E., "Mental Health and the Family,"

Journal of Marriage and Family, Vol. 29, No. 1, 1967, pp. 18-39.

Watzlawick, Paul, "A Structured Family Interview," *Family Process*, Vol. 5, No. 2, 1966, pp. 256-271.

Wilkinson, C., and C. Reed, "An Approach to the Family Therapy Process," *Diseases of the Nervous System*, Vol. 26, 1965, pp. 705-714.

Winnicott, D. W., *The Family and Individual Development*, Tavistock, 1965.

Zuk, Gerald H., "Family Therapy," *Archives of General Psychiatry*, Vol. 16, 1967, pp. 71-79.

Zuk, Gerald H., "On the Pathology of Silencing Strategies," *Family Process*, Vol. 4, No. 1, March 1965, pp. 32-49.

Zuk, Gerald H., "The Go-Between Process in Family Therapy," *Family Process*, Vol. 5, No. 2, September 1966, pp. 162-178.

Indices for Individual or Conjoint Therapy

Charney, Israel W., "Integrated Individual and Family Psychotherapy," *Family Process*, Vol. 5, No. 2, 1966, pp. 179-198.

Feldman, Marvin J., "Privacy and Conjoint Family Therapy," *Family Process*, Vol. 6, No. 1, 1967, pp. 1-9.

Fleck, S., "Some General and Specific Indications for Family Therapy," *Confinia Psychiatry*, Vol. 8, 1965, pp. 27-36.

Fox, Ronald E., Ph.D., "The Effects of Psychotherapy on the Spouse," *Family Process*, Vol. 7, No. 1, March 1968, pp. 7-16.

Sherman, Sanford N., "Family Treatment: An Approach to Children's Problems," *Social Casework*, Vol. 47, No. 6, June 1966, pp. 368-372.

Wildman, M., "Communication in Family Therapy," *British Journal of Psychiatric Social Work*, Vol. IX, No. 2, 1967.

Williams, Frank S., M.D., "Family Therapy: A Critical Assessment," *American Journal of Orthopsychiatry*, Vol. 37, No. 5, October 1967, pp. 912-949.

The Training and Role of the Counselor

Ackerman, Nathan, "Family Psychotherapy - Theory and Practice," *American Journal of Psychotherapy*, Vol. 20, December 1966, pp. 405-414.

Ailen, Monroe S., "Conjoint Therapy and the Corrective Emotional Experience," *Family Process*, Vol. 5, No. 1, March 1966, pp. 91-104.

Curry, Andrew E., "The Family Therapy Situation as a System," *Family Process*, Vol. 5, No. 2, September 1966, pp. 131-141.

Dwyer, John H., M.D., Mildred Menk, and Carol Van Houten, "The Caseworker's Role in Family Therapy with Severely Disturbed Children," *Family Process*, Vol. 4, No. 1, March 1965, pp. 21-31.

Gehrke, Shirley, and Marvin Kirschenbaum, "Survival Patterns in Conjoint Family Therapy," *Family Process*, Vol. 6, No. 1, 1967, pp. 67-80.

Hansen, Constance C., ACSW, "An Extended Home Visit With Conjoint Family Therapy," *Family Process*, Vol. 7, No. 1, March 1968, pp. 67-87.

Howell, D., and P. Parsloe, "Working with a Family in a Child Guidance Setting," *British Journal of Psychiatric Social Work*, Vol. 8, No. 4, 1966.

Humiston, Karl E., M.D., "Family Therapy: Some Contributions to Treatment and Training," *Hospital and Community Psychiatry*, Vol. 18, 1967, pp. 40-43.

Landes, Judah, and William Winter, "A New Strategy for Treating Disintegrated Families," *Family Process*, Vol. 5, No. 1, March 1966, pp. 1-20.

Laskin, Eva R., Ph.D., "Breaking Down the Walls," *Family Process*, Vol. 7, No. 1, March 1968, pp. 118-125.

Lefer, J., "Counter-Resistance in Family Therapy," *Journal of Hillside Hospital*, Vol. 15, 1966, pp. 205-210.

Mitchell, Celia B., "Integrative Therapy of the Family

Unit," *Social Casework*, Vol. 46, No. 2, February 1965, pp. 63-69.

Rabkin, Leslie, "Sources of Strain in the Treatment of Disturbed Children and Their Families," *Mental Hygiene*, Vol. 49, No. 4, October 1965, pp. 544-548.

Sherman, Sanford N., "Aspects of Family Interviewing Critical for Staff Training and Education," *Social Service Review*, Vol. 40, No. 3, September 1966, pp. 302-308.

Smordan, Lawrence E., "The Use of Drama in Teaching Family Relationships," *Journal of Marriage and Family*, Vol. 28, No. 2, 1966, pp. 219-223.

Sonne, John C., M.D., and Geraldine Lincoln, M.Ed., "Heterosexual Co-Therapy Team Experiences During Family Therapy," *Family Process*, Vol. 4, No. 2, September 1965, pp. 177-197.

Zuk, Gerald, "When the Family Therapist Takes Sides: A Case Report," *Psychotherapy: Theory, Research and Practice*, Vol. 5, No. 1, 1968, pp. 24-28.

Family Diagnosis and Treatment

Friedman, Alfred *et al*, *Psychotherapy for the Whole Family*, New York - Springer Publication Company, 1965.

Earle, John R., "Parent-Child Communication, Sentiment, and Authority," *Sociological Inquiry*, Vol. 37, No. 2, Spring 1967, pp. 275-282.

Jensen, Gordon D., and John G. Wallace, "Family Mourning Process," *Family Process*, Vol. 6, No. 1, March 1967.

Langsley, Donald G., M.D., Robert W. Fairbarin, M.D., and Carol DeYoung, R.N., "Adolescence and Family Crises," *Canadian Psychiatric Association Journal*, Vol. 13, No. 2, April 1968, pp. 125-135.

Nulfi, Mary W., "Families in Grief: The Question of Casework Intervention," *Social Work*, Vol. 12, No. 4, October 1967, pp. 40-46.

Paul, Norman L., and George H. Grosser, "Operational Mourning and Its Role in Conjoint Family Therapy," *Community Mental Health Journal*, Vol. 1, No. 4, 1965, pp. 339-345.

Schulman, Gerda, and Elsa Leichter, "The Prevention of Family Break-Up," *Social Casework*, Vol. 49, No. 3, March 1968, pp. 143-150.

Wasser, Edna, "Family Casework Focus on the Older Person," *Social Casework*, Vol. 47, No. 7, July 1966, pp. 423-429.

Tharp, Roland G., "Marriage Roles, Child Development and Family Treatment," *American Journal of Orthopsychiatry*, Vol. 35, No. 3, April 1965, pp. 531-538.

Problems Relating to Socio-Economic Status

Billingsley, Andrew, and Amy Billingsley, "Negro Family Life in America," *Social Service Review*, Vol. 39, No. 4, December 1965, pp. 310-319.

Bittermann, Catherine M., "The Multimarriage Family," *Social Casework*, Vol. 49, No. 4, April 1968, pp. 218-221.

Chope, M. D., and Lilian Blackford, "The Chronic Problem Family: San Mateo County's Experience," *American Journal of Orthopsychiatry*, Vol. 33, No. 3, 1963, pp. 462-469.

Ferreira, Antonio J., "Psychosis and Family Myth," *American Journal of Psychotherapy*, Vol. 21, 1967, pp. 186-197.

King, Charles, "Family Therapy with the Deprived Family," *Social Casework*, Vol. 48, No. 4, April 1967, pp. 203-208.

Kushner, Sylvia, "The Divorced, Non-Custodial Parent and Family Treatment," *Social Work*, Vol. 10, No. 3, July 1965, pp. 52-58.

Menzies, Malbert, M.D., "The Angry Parent in Family Oriented Therapy," *Canadian Psychiatric Association Journal*, Vol. 10, 1965, pp. 405-410.

Miller, Daniel R., Ph.D., and Jack C. Westman, M.D., "Family Teamwork and Psychotherapy," *Family Process*, Vol. 5, No. 1, March 1966, pp. 49-59.

Minuchin, Salvador, "Conflict-Resolution Family Therapy," *Psychiatry*, Vol. 28, No. 3, August 1965, pp. 278-286.

JL

Minuchin, Salvador, and Braulio Montalvo, "Techniques for Working With Disorganized, Low Socio-Economic Families," *American Journal of Orthopsychiatry*, Vol. XXXVII, No. 5, October 1967, pp. 880-887.

Minuchin, Salvador, Braulio Montalvo, Bernard G. Guerney, Jr., Bernice L. Rosman, and Florence Schumer, *Families in the Slums, An Exploration of Their Structure and Treatment*, New York, Basic Books, 1967.

Ryan, Francis, "Clarifying Some Issues in Family Group Casework," *Social Casework*, Vol. 48, No. 4, April 1967, pp. 222-226.

Travisono, Anthony P., and Carle F. O'Neil, "Intromitive Family Therapy," *Corrective Psychiatry and Journal of Social Therapy*, Vol. 12, No. 3, May 1966, pp. 229-237.

Footnotes

[1]. Excerpted from **Family Dynamics: A Survey of the Literature 1965-1968**, prepared with the support of U.S.P.H.S., NIMH Grant No.5 T01 MH 07982-07, Student Research Stipends by Elizabeth A. Quick and Julia F. Walker under the supervision of the program director for the Grant, Dr. Leon Lucas.